Breaking and Schooling

Breaking and Schooling

Carolyn Henderson
and
Lynn Russell

SWAN HILL
PRESS

DEDICATION

This book is in memory of Susan Vennard, with
love and admiration.

Photo Credit

All the photographs were supplied by John Henderson.

First published in the UK in 1994
by Swan Hill Press
an imprint of Airlife Publishing Ltd

British Library Cataloguing in Publication Data
  A catalogue record for this book
  is available from the British Library

ISBN 1 85310 472 8

Typeset by Hewer Text Composition Services, Edinburgh
Printed by Butler & Tanner Ltd, Frome and London.

Swan Hill Press
an imprint of Airlife Publishing Ltd
101 Longden Road, Shrewsbury SY3 9EB

Contents

Introduction

Training horses is a subject surrounded by mystique. In one way this is understandable, because the transformation of an unbroken youngster or an ignorant older animal into an obedient, well-schooled ride is a fascinating and rewarding challenge. But training is not the province of a chosen few: anyone who can ride competently and has his or her fair share of common sense has the potential to become an effective trainer.

We are not talking about producing Grand Prix dressage horses or Grade A show jumpers, though you might be lucky enough to find that you have a potential star. The aim of this book is to help you turn your raw material (whether promising or decidedly otherwise!) into a horse who is a pleasure to own and ride. Riding is, after all, meant to be fun – and whether you compete or simply enjoy hacking out, you want a horse to be responsive and in balance.

Many riders who are perfectly capable of breaking a youngster or re-educating an older horse are reluctant to try, because they are frightened of spoiling the horse. As long as you have time, patience, adequate facilities and if necessary someone to help in a crisis, you can stop worrying. Everyone makes mistakes, even the most experienced trainers; as long as you recognise when things have gone wrong and go back a few steps to put them right, everything will be fine.

You are only human and your horse is only – a horse. There will be times when you explain things the wrong way and he does not understand. There will also be times when you explain things the right way and he understands, but does not do what you ask. Sometimes it will be because he cannot manage it, perhaps because he is at that point physically incapable of it. Sometimes it will be because he is fed up or distracted by outside influences such as other horses, windy weather or too much good food.

There will be times when you get to the verge of losing your temper because there is a total communication breakdown. If you can recognise this, count to ten and try a different approach, you have no reason to worry about your capability as a trainer. Most riders, even the best ones, occasionally blow a fuse, hit a horse and then regret it: the danger comes if this is more than an isolated occurrence. Trainers need to be patient, but they also need to be stubborn and occasionally bloody minded!

Anyone who can handle horses correctly can teach a youngster its basic manners – how to lead, tie up, have its feet picked up and so on. Early riding demands someone who can stay in balance when the horse sticks its head in the air, acts as if it has three legs instead of four or does any of the other things young horses do. The rider must be effective and be able to help the horse when he needs it, which is not always the same as keeping a textbook position.

Ride lots of different horses before you decide to try and train one from scratch. It is no coincidence that some of the best training riders are those who work in dealers' yards, where the turnover is rapid and, because time is a luxury, the results often have to be equally fast. This does not mean that horses are not broken and schooled properly, rather that professionals know when and how to take shortcuts. The 'average' owner has the advantage of not having to work against the clock and can progress at a pace to suit both horse and trainer.

If you have never trained a horse before, you will need help from someone who has. This book will steer you along the right lines, but unfortunately horses cannot read and do not always behave as you expect them to. Your helper should have honest to goodness hands-on experience: with all due respect to the many talented instructors with professional qualifications, letters after your name do not make you a trainer of horses.

If you want to specialise in a particular discipline, be it dressage, show jumping, showing or whatever, go to someone who is successful in producing horses for that field. You would not ask a plumber to put a new roof on your house, so why ask a dressage rider to help you produce your show jumper? Good trainers all have the same aims in mind – a horse that goes forward freely and in balance – but different jobs demand different approaches.

To train a horse, you must have some basic facilities. This does not necessarily mean an international size arena, set of BSJA show jumps and your own cross-country course. What is essential is a reasonably flat, enclosed area for lungeing and schooling and the company of a sensible rider on an equally sensible and reliable horse to act as schoolmaster and escort for early rides out. You will also need a helper on the ground: this does not have to be an experienced rider, but must be someone who is calm and used to handling horses and judging their reactions.

However competent and experienced you are, it is potentially dangerous to introduce a horse to new experiences when you are on your own. The quietest, most laid-back animal is quite capable of doing a Jekyll and Hyde – and sometimes they do it at the things you think are least likely to bother them. The emphasis should always be on prevention rather than cure, and throughout this book there is advice on common traps and how not to fall into them.

It is not meant to sound as if training horses should carry a government health warning, rather that it is better for your sake and the horse's to play safe. Horses learn unproductive lessons just as quickly as productive ones; there will undoubtedly be a few times when you have to work through a disagreement, but there will be lots more when confrontations can be avoided.

This book falls into two sections. The first covers training a horse from scratch up to backing and early riding, and the second deals with more advanced work and problems that can arise at later stages. Even if you break the horse from scratch, you are likely to have some hiccups – again, life would be a lot easier if the horse could read this book instead of you!

Timetables have been avoided deliberately. Guidelines are offered sometimes to help you plan the horse's work, but they are suggestions rather than rigid rules. Aim to progress quickly by all means, but do not fall into the trap of thinking 'The book says that by the tenth week we should be doing A B and C' and worrying because you have only managed A and B. Your horse will find some things easier than others, so do not worry if you hit patches where you seem to be standing still (or even worse, going backwards!) rather than making steady progress.

If you are training a youngster, you will be able to give him an all-round education so that he ends up with good manners on the ground as well as under saddle. But if your pupil is an older animal who has not been taught the basics, you will have to instil them as part of your training programme. A horse can be nice to ride but a pig on the ground; it is easier to teach a yearling to lead, tie up etc than a pushy, mature horse who has learned to throw his weight around – but it can be done.

No horse is a push button ride all of the time . . . and if he was, he would probably be very boring. And because horses are just as individual as people, there may be times when you have to solve a problem or hang-up that may or may not be your fault. Training is a continual process and it is never too late to improve the way a horse goes.

There is a special chapter on re-schooling ex-racehorses – the wastage rate in the Thoroughbred industry has been estimated at around a horrifying 75 per cent. The ones that stay sound can often be re-routed successfully to other careers: many have gone on to become top class eventers, show jumpers and show horses. Their early education for racing leaves them with a peculiar mixture of pluses and minuses, but if you know what to expect you can end up with a really nice horse.

The secrets of successful training are to work out what you want the horse to do and to explain that to him in a way he can understand: as a successful trainer of novice show jumpers once said, 'training is just a series of repeated aids.' There are no magic wands or secret formulae, though you will find plenty of tips that stop you making mistakes.

There will be days when you make breakthroughs and days when you seem to take one step forwards and two steps back. But you will never be bored – and when you can enjoy riding your horse, knowing that you have shaped his education from scratch or from an unpromising beginning, you will have a sense of achievement that nothing can match.

Part One
Breaking

Chapter 1
Buying a Youngster

If you are buying a young horse as opposed to bringing on a homebred animal, the first thing you have to decide is what age group to go for. All have advantages and disadvantages, but if you buy a foal or a yearling you have two or three years ahead of you before you can even think about starting ridden work. That is not to say that you cannot have a lot of fun – and if you start with a horse in that age group, you know that there is less risk of having to sort out someone else's mistakes. The other side of the coin is, of course, that any problems will be down to you!

As far as the initial purchase price goes, a foal will usually be the cheapest option. But if you are brave enough to sit down and work out how much it will cost you to keep him until he is rideable, it may well work out more expensive than buying a two- or three-year-old.

The advantage of buying a foal from its breeder is that you can see its dam and sometimes its sire and be able to assess temperament and conformation. You may also be able to see other stock from the same combination, which will give you an idea of the way your foal is likely to develop. But inevitably, buying a foal is always something of a gamble. You can make an educated guess at its eventual height, temperament etc, but may still get a surprise (pleasant or otherwise.) A lot of things can change – even the foal's colour!

Some breeders say their stock is so much in demand that they can 'sell' foals before they are born to purchasers who are willing to pay a deposit without seeing the result. This is not usually an acceptable risk: by all means be prepared to pay a deposit to reserve a foal at weaning, but make sure that there is a written agreement on the terms of the deposit and the conditions on which it could be refunded to avoid any misunderstandings.

It takes a lot of skill to look at a newborn foal and decide whether or not it will grow to match your expectations. All foals are appealing and all are long legged and wobbly – but by the time it has got through its first week it should be straight limbed, steady on its feet and bold enough to investigate its surroundings.

Look at the mare (and if you get the chance, at the stallion) as hard as you look at their offspring. Both should have good temperaments; this is just as important as good conformation. There is no such thing as the perfect horse, but beware of glaring conformation faults in either parent and look very carefully at the foal to see if it has inherited them (see the guidelines later in this chapter).

All foals are appealing – but look for good limbs and a bold outlook.

Fortunately there is a move away from the old practice of breeding from a mare just because she has been with the owners for a long time and they are fond of her – or even worse, breeding from her because they cannot think what else to do with her. To put it bluntly, if you breed from the mediocre you are likely to end up with the mediocre.

Both mare and stallion should be well made and preferably have proved themselves in terms of performance; do not reject a foal if the dam has not done anything, provided she meets the other criteria and provided the sire has proved or is proving that he has the ability in your chosen sphere as well as the looks. Again, there is a growing and welcome move in this country towards performance stallions: horses who are intended to be sires of dressage horses, show jumpers or eventers are having to prove that they can do the job themselves.

By the time the foal has become a yearling, he or she has come through the crucial first winter and will be looking more like a horse in the making and less like a cuddly toy. Gender is purely a matter of choice and many buyers would be advised to remember that a good mare often has an extra sparkle that a gelding may lack. If injury cuts short her ridden career and she is good enough to breed from, she also has a future there.

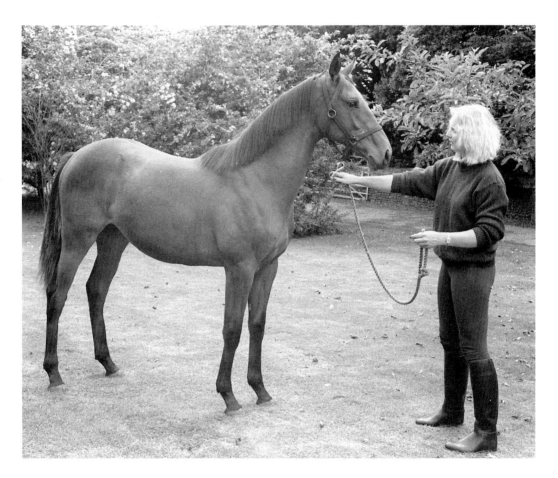

A well-made yearling filly by a Thoroughbred stallion out of a hunter mare. When this picture was taken, she was recovering from a hindleg injury . . . buying a youngster is just as much a risk as buying an older animal.

If you are interested in showing, you can also have a lot of fun showing yearlings and above in hand. This is often a controversial area, because too many undeveloped horses in the show ring still carry too much bodyweight and run the risk of limb deformities.

Top producers know that a horse in show condition is very different from a horse that is fat: unfortunately the message still has to get through to the lower rungs of the ladder.

Many people opt for a two- or three-year-old, because there is less time to wait before it can start learning to be a 'proper horse' and it has gone through at least some of the ugly duckling stage. It has to be said, though, that there is no guarantee that you are going to end up with a swan: there may still be times when you look at your two-year-old, wondering if the front end will ever match the back and why on earth you were optimistic enough to buy it in the first place.

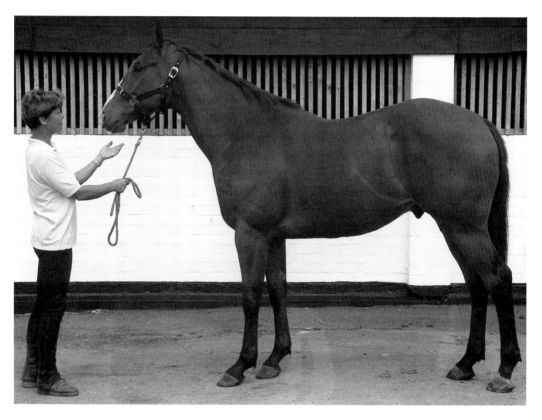

A three-year-old Thoroughbred who combines quality and substance and is a great event prospect.

A lot of youngsters are now sold through the auction ring. Many of the better class sales have shrugged off any kind of dubious image – in fact some of them have become positively prestigious, with prices to match. Do not assume that a horse has been entered in a sale because it has a problem (it may, but then again so may many of those advertised through 'normal' channels!) Some experienced trainers are quite happy to buy from sales, because they believe that seeing a youngster's reactions to a new, exciting and stressful environment can tell them a lot about its temperament and character. Most youngsters are confident in home surroundings, but the one that comes up to you boldly, with ears pricked, in a strange place has the right sort of outlook for any job.

Whatever age you decide on, be realistic about your ability and your ambitions. Although many Thoroughbred or nearly Thoroughbred horses have excellent temperaments, they have quick reactions. A halfbred horse with a nice temperament is often an easier prospect for someone taking on a youngster for the first time – and if you are buying a youngster purely as an interesting project, why not think about a pony?

A pony will be cheaper to buy, cheaper to keep and usually easier to handle. There are exceptions: a wild three-year-old straight off the moor, who has never been handled, may tax every ounce of your patience and ingenuity. But a well handled native pony from a good stud will give you just as much experience as a horse, will probably cause less damage to your bank balance and be easy to sell on if you do a good job on his breaking and early riding.

It is equally important to make sure that you can provide a youngster with the right environment: not always easy if you intend to keep him at livery. It is essential that young horses spend most of their time at grass, and that it be good quality land with good fencing and adequate shelter. It is not on to confine a young horse to a box for 23 hours out of 24 (in fact it is not on to keep any horse in those conditions, but that is another story.)

He must also have equine company, either from roughly the same age group or from at least one old, steady animal. The hurly burly of the average DIY grass livery set-up, where you get a mixture of ages and sexes, can cause problems. It is all very well to say that age groups mix in the wild, but it is not quite the same. For a start, none of the horses have shoes on. A youngster who irritates the older horses may easily get kicked.

Finally, do you have the time, the patience and the money to keep and bring on a youngster? Do not fall into the common trap of thinking that a youngster is cheaper to keep than an older horse because all you have to do is turn him out until he is three. He will still need feeding correctly, worming and innoculating. He will also need regular attention from the farrier and to have his teeth looked at and when necessary rasped by your horse dentist or vet.

Assessing the youngster

Most people buy young horses hoping that they will grow up to do a particular job. Looking at a weanling or a yearling and trying to work out if it will make an event or show jumping prospect is always a gamble, because until you get to the stage where you can try it over fences you have to rely on conformation, temperament, breeding – and luck. Potential dressage and show horses are easier to spot in that you can see the quality (or otherwise) of movement from the start, but again you sometimes have to keep your fingers crossed that you have bought an ugly duckling that will turn into a swan rather than just an ugly duck.

Breeding is down to personal preferences and prejudices and whether or not you want to be influenced by fashion. Whilst all horses are individuals, the different breeds have characteristics in temperament and conformation that can work for you or against you. As Britain becomes more aware of the importance of bloodlines, the two- or three-year-old of 'unknown breeding' will become less common. It is always nice to know a horse's parentage, but no one with common sense would turn down a horse with good conformation, movement and temperament because of his lack of a family tree.

Whatever job the horse is intended for, good conformation is vital if he is to stay sound and achieve his maximum athletic potential. The perfect horse has yet to be born (and if you insist on trying to find him you are in for a long wait) but if you look at the top performers you will see very few with glaringly bad conformation. There will always be the occasional freak who breaks all the rules, but they are few and far between.

In many ways, the most important part of a horse is the one you cannot see – the bit between the ears. A good brain and bold, generous temperament can make up for a lot of defects. There are successful horses with suspect temperaments, but they are inevitably in the hands of professionals who have the time and experience necessary. And even they sometimes decide that it is not worth it!

Very few horses are born nasty, but some are made that way by incorrect handling. However, some horses are naturally confident and curious about anything new, whereas others tend to be doubtful and a bit nervous at first – rather like people. Obviously a lot depends on how much (and how well) a youngster has been handled, but you can still tell a lot from the way he reacts when you approach him.

Does he prick up his ears with interest and look at you, or is he tense and poised for flight? Is he happy for you to be near him, or does he lay back his ears (or even worse, try and kick or bite) because you are invading what he considers is his territory?

Conformation is not just about looking pretty. It is about a symmetry of frame that gives the horse the best possible chance of standing up to the incredible strain we put him under – and it starts at ground level. 'No foot, no horse' is a saying that is as true today as it ever was. If a horse has good feet and limbs you can forgive it a lot of other minus points. A handsome head may be a wonderful sight to see over your stable door, but it will not help your horse stay sound.

If you bring it down to facts and figures, it is a wonder that so many horses stay sound. When all four feet are on the ground, you get 500-600kg (plus the weight of the rider) borne on a surface area of about 600 sq cms. At times, the weight is borne on one foot – and when the horse lands over a jump, there is a period when a single limb has to take a force equivalent to many times the horse's bodyweight.

The first thing to notice is whether front and back feet each make a pair. The back feet are usually slightly narrower than the front ones, but in each case the near foot should look as if it is a partner to the one on the offside. If one is noticeably bigger than the other, be careful: a contracted foot is often, though not always, a sign of a problem. The sole should ideally be slightly concave rather than flat – though a tendency to flat feet is common in horses with Irish Draught blood.

The pasterns should be neither too upright nor too sloping; hind pasterns are slightly shorter than the front ones. If they are too short and upright, the horse will be uncomfortable to ride because he will not have the correct 'shock absorbing' conformation; even more important, he will be susceptible to problems such as ringbone that are often related to concussion. Horses with pasterns that are too long may be a comfortable ride, but because the fetlocks drop down too far with each stride, extra strain is put on tendons and ligaments.

When you look at the horse from the front, the measurement between the centres of his hooves should be about the same as that between the points of the shoulder. If it is greater – which often happens with narrow chested horses – he is base wide, which can put greater strain on the inside of the forelegs and feet. If it is smaller, you have the opposite side of the coin and the horse is base narrow. In this case the outsides of the limbs and feet bear more of the brunt than they should.

Forearms should be long and cannon bones should be short, again to help the horse cope most effectively with work. Avoid the horse who is markedly over or back at the knee, faults which put extra strain on the tendons. (Over at the knee means that there is a concave outline between the base of the knee and the top of the fetlock; back at the knee means that the outline is convex.) Look at the horse from the front: his cannon bones should come straight down from the knees, not be offset.

All the joints – knees, fetlocks and hocks – should look as if they are pairs and should be hard and flat, with no signs of puffiness. The hock joints are perhaps the most important of all, because they are the site of the horse's 'engine'. When you stand behind him, you should be able to drop imaginary perpendicular lines from the points of the buttocks to bisect hocks, cannon bones and heels. Avoid the horse with sickle hocks, where the leg is in front of a perpendicular dropped from the point of the hock to the ground. This conformation makes it hard for the horse to collect himself and push off the ground, so is a big minus for both dressage horses and jumpers.

Cow hocks, where the hocks turn inwards, are less of a problem unless the fault is very pronounced. Ginny Elliot (neé Leng) admits that Master Craftsman, perhaps her best ever horse, was cow hocked – but it did not do him much harm!

An older horse who has worked hard may show signs of wear and tear such as splints. They may often be acceptable faults, unless you are looking for a show horse. It is a different story with a young horse: if his joints and limbs show signs of wear at such an early age, when he should not have done anything worth speaking of, how can he be expected to stand up to work later on?

If the feet and limbs stand up to scrutiny, it is worth looking at the rest. In theory we hope to see a harmonious picture where all the components make up a whole: in practice, assessing this can be harder than it sounds when you are looking at a growing youngster with one end higher than the other! Even so, it is possible to look past the gawkiness and form a reasonable idea of how the horse will look when he matures.

Although the shape of a horse's head is not important in itself, it can give you an idea of his breeding and character. A lot of people will tell you to look for a large, generous eye as an indicator of a good temperament, but this is not always the case. In the same way, showing the whites of the eyes is not necessarily a sign that the horse is wild: it is simply that some have more white than others. The one thing that does seem to be significant is that a lot of horses who have pronounced bumps between their eyes have awkward temperaments to go with them – though again, there are exceptions to every rule.

Look in the horse's mouth, even if he is only a weanling. If his jaw conformation is incorrect, he may have problems eating or accepting the bit. The upper and lower incisors should meet more or less evenly and not be badly overshot or undershot. The first, also called 'parrot mouth', means that the upper jaw is too long; the second means that the upper jaw is too short. Both conditions can make it more difficult for the horse to eat, though this depends on their severity.

A short necked horse may make you feel that there is nothing in front of you when you sit on him, but may be a fault you can live with. Ewe necks – which look as if they have been put on upside down – are far worse. Horses with this conformation cannot flex properly and often go with hollow backs, making for an uncomfortable ride. If the fault is there, no amount of schooling will put it right.

A horse with a nice sloping shoulder will be a more comfortable ride and should in theory stay sound longer: an upright shoulder usually goes with upright pasterns, and an up and down, jarring action that sends a shock through the limbs with every stride.

The horse who is reasonably compact will usually find it easier to balance himself, provided that he has no glaring faults to offset it. Long backs tend to be a sign of weakness, though remember that mares are usually longer in the back than geldings. There is no reason why a horse with a slightly long back cannot be a great athlete, but it will take a lot of work and plenty of transitions and half halts to get him working from behind in a round outline.

It is always nice if the horse has a deep girth, as this gives more room for the heart and lungs and thus gives greater potential for stamina. Herring gutted horses, who always look 'run up' like a greyhound, are difficult to keep condition on. They usually need a breastplate or breastgirth – but if everything else is right, there is no reason why the horse cannot be a good athlete.

The hindquarters are important, because they form part of the horse's 'engine' – but the area behind the saddle can be built up with correct work and feeding. The ideal from the aesthetic point of view, and therefore for the show horse, is a flat, broad croup and well set-on tail. However, a goose rump – where there is a bump at the top of the quarters – is said to be a sign of jumping ability and so could sometimes be a plus rather than a minus!

Trying to keep all this in mind while looking at a gangly, leggy youngster may seem difficult, but you should still get the impression of a series of flowing lines rather than sharp angles. A lot of people find it hard to judge conformation at this stage, because the horse has such a lot of growing to do, but the basics will not change. A short neck will not miraculously lengthen, and a yearling that is so narrow chested that both legs look to come out of the same hole will be the same as a three-year-old.

Common sense will usually enable you to predict a youngster's eventual height with reasonable accuracy, but if the sire and dam are of very different heights you could be in for a (not always pleasant!) surprise. Research shows that it is the mare's body size which determines the eventual height of the foal, but as a rough guide, a Thoroughbred foal's birthweight will be about 10 per cent of its adult weight. By the time a young horse reaches his first birthday he will have achieved about 65 per cent of his final adult bodyweight and about 90 per cent of his height – so anyone who presents you with a 13hh yearling and tells you that he is bound to make 16.2hh is being rather optimistic.

Movement and conformation usually go hand in hand. In an ideal world, straight, rhythmic paces are preferable whatever job you are going to ask the horse to do – and if you are looking for a show horse, good movement is essential. If a horse moves straight, he will be less likely to injure himself by, for instance, knocking one leg against the other (brushing).

However, you only have to look at horses competing in top level competition to realise that perfect movement is not always essential – even for dressage. That might sound far fetched, but watch horses competing at Grand Prix level and you will see more than one who turns a toe slightly or goes a little close behind. The same applies to eventing and show jumping: if a horse leaves the fences up, it does not matter if his movement would not win him prizes in the show ring.

It is always a matter of degree. The horse who turns a toe is very different from the one who dishes in an exaggerated way from the shoulder, and puts strain on the whole limb. Similarly, the horse who moves close behind can be protected against the odd knock by putting boots on him, but the one who knocks his fetlocks at every stride will inevitably suffer the consequences.

When you assess a horse's movement you are checking to see that he is sound as well as looking at the quality of his paces. He must be on a loose leadrope or rein so that he has the freedom to move naturally: clever handlers can disguise quite a bit by holding the horse's head in and running him up at a slight angle.

Start by standing behind him and watching him walk away. A lot of people only bother to watch a horse trot, but racehorse trainers say that a long striding, generous walk that overtracks by four to eight inches means that a horse can gallop. Then watch him in trot; make the handler earn his money by trotting him four times, if possible, so that you can watch him from behind, in front and from both sides. This is the pace in which any unsoundness or deviations from straightness will show up: how much importance you place on them depends on the horse's other plus and minus points and his future career.

Horses for courses

One man's meat is another man's poison, and that is certainly true of horses. When you are buying an unbroken horse in the hope that he will do a specialised job, you have to accept that there is a fair amount of luck involved – though you can make sure that the odds are in your favour. Unless you are either 100 per cent sure of your own judgement, or are prepared to gamble, avoid buying a youngster with really marked defects in conformation or movement: a horse that has everything in all the right places will always find a buyer for another job, even if he turns out not to be suitable for yours. But if your would-be Grade A with a ewe neck turns out to have a fear of heights, his conformation will not help him find favour elsewhere (at least, not at a price that helps compensate for the time and money you have spent on him.)

Dressage

Dressage is influenced by fashion perhaps more than any other sport. A few years ago, it was accepted that you had to ride a big warmblood with extravagant movement to get anywhere at the higher levels – which was unfortunate if you happened to be small and light. Now there is a return to lightness and grace rather than power and dominance; warmbloods are still popular, because of their good paces and generally amenable temperaments, but the modern warmblood tends to show more Thoroughbred influence.

A dressage horse has to take a lot of pressure, so a good temperament is vital. There are very few Thoroughbreds competing at top level; a good Thoroughbred is a wonderful horse, but he is bred for speed rather than the disciplines and confines of the dressage arena. His conformation is designed to help him go fast, so he may find it difficult to achieve the high level of collection needed for advanced work.

Look for a horse whose conformation means that he was naturally 'born on the bit' and you will give yourself a head start. The dressage horse should have a well-developed hindleg; it is sometimes said that slight sickle hocks are not a disadvantage, as they give the impression that the horse is putting his back legs underneath himself, but to be honest this is a form of cynicism that does not work. You might fool some people, but you will not fool any judge worth his or her salt.

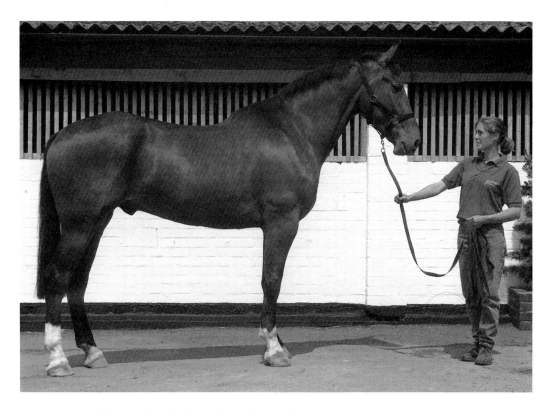

A three-year-old warmblood whose future lies in dressage or show jumping.

A correctly set-on head and neck and a good turn through the neck and throat (as opposed to being thick through the jowl) make it easier for a horse to come on to the bit. Look for a good slope to the shoulder; the horse who is upright will be less rhythmic in his paces and will find it hard to lengthen. Good movement is, of course, desirable – but rhythm and a stride which comes from the shoulder, coupled with a slight turn of the toe, are preferable to a horse which moves technically straight but has a choppy stride.

As with all disciplines, colour comes last in the list of priorities. But as with showing, a stunning grey or flashy chestnut can liven up a procession of boring bays – and judges are only human! Some riders believe that markings can cause an unfortunate optical illusion – for instance, that one white sock can give the impression that the horse is not straight – but it really depends on your degree of paranoia.

You will be striving to present a harmonious picture, so you need a horse that suits you. If you are small and slim, a 16hh lightweight, elegant horse will look far more in keeping than a 17.2hh warmblood.

Show jumping

Show jumpers come in all shapes and sizes, but extremes are rare; the 14.2hh Strollers and the 18hh mountains are few and far between. Professionals do not care how big or how small a horse is as long as he leaves the poles up, but remember that very big horses are usually harder to keep together and find it more difficult to turn sharply. Be realistic in your ambitions: a 15.2hh might not manage the huge spreads of a Grade A course, but are you really likely to get that far? A 15.2hh with a bit of ability should manage Newcomers and Foxhunter courses and be handier with it. Tall riders will obviously want a bigger horse, but do not over-horse yourself in the mistaken impression that nothing under 16.2hh can do the job.

When looking at youngsters, look for a good back end. Even though it will be undeveloped, you want to see powerful hocks and a nice length of second thigh. Good limbs and feet are as important as ever; watch a horse landing over a fence and look at the stress he has to absorb.

Few show jumpers will turn down a prospect because he dishes, but many will avoid a toe-flicking 'daisy cutter'. Instead, they look for a trot with a slightly rounder action, as the horse that moves this way usually picks his feet up over a pole.

The Continental fashion of loose-jumping young horses and even foals is catching on here. A youngster who has a natural bold, careful jump when loose will inevitably give you more confidence than one which is as happy to go through the poles as round them. Having said that, there are also horses who jump in spectacular fashion when loose-schooled but are much less impressive with a rider on board.

Eventing

The top class advanced event horse is nearly always Thoroughbred and may well have started his working life in a racing yard. (See chapter 13 for the advantages and disadvantages this may bring.) The Thoroughbred has the speed and stamina no other breeding can match; some riders feel that a seven-eighths-bred acquires a bit of native cunning and the ability to find a 'fifth leg' when necessary from its dash of pony or hunter blood.

Again, be realistic. If your ambitions centre on pre-novice, novice or intermediate level, you will certainly be on course with a good three-quarter-bred or even half-bred. Geldings predominate in the sport (unlike show jumping, where few leading riders have the same prejudices as their eventing counterparts) but there are a few hopeful signs that mares are making their mark in horse trials, too. It certainly makes sense: the risk of injury must be higher and a mare who has proved herself in competition has a profitable future as a brood mare.

An event horse has to be brave, so avoid the 'shy violets' when looking at youngsters. A bold but kind outlook is essential; if the brain is not right to start with, it will certainly blow a fuse when the mature horse is eventing fit and under pressure in the dressage arena. Good limbs and feet are also top priorities – if you buy a horse out of training, do not touch anything that has or has shown any sign of tendon injury, as there is a high risk of the horse breaking down.

In theory you are looking for the impossible: a horse that combines all the qualities of the dressage horse and show jumper plus stamina, speed and courage. In practice, most riders put cross-country jumping ability first and hope that they can sort out the rest. Dressage is now a much more influential phase than it used to be, but an equable temperament is more important than mouth-watering paces: accuracy and freedom from tension count for a lot on the marks sheets.

Show jumping is many event riders' bugbear, but this can be because they find it hard to adapt to the confines of the jumping arena. Even at top level, the show jumping fences are a maximum four feet one inch (1.25m). In pre-novice classes, you are talking about a maximum three feet seven inches (1.10m). This should be within the potential reach of any athletic youngster.

Chapter 2
Settling In

Once you have found your horse of the future, it is a good idea to have him vetted before handing over your money. A lot of people assume that vetting is a waste of money, because the horse will not have had time to develop problems, but this attitude can be a quick way to lose a lot of money. Waiting two or three years to ride your horse, only to discover that he has an eye or heart defect that means he will not stand up to work, is heartbreaking; it might not happen very often, but why take the chance at all?

It is also important to insure your new purchase for vets' fees. Youngsters are often accident prone, because they are inquisitive and playful. Most accidents are thankfully minor ones, but if the worst happens and your horse injures himself so badly that he needs an operation, veterinary fee cover means you can afford to give him the best chance of recovery. As with all insurance, read the small print in the policy carefully – for instance, some companies exclude any claims arising during the first week or fortnight of ownership.

With all the precautions out of the way, you can look forward to bringing your new youngster home. Do everything you can to make the move as stress-free as possible; this will be the most traumatic period the horse will ever have been through, perhaps even more so than weaning. After up to three years in the same environment, with the same equine and human companions, you are uprooting him to a strange place where nothing is familiar.

It is a bonus if he has travelled in a horsebox before and has been taught to load and unload without fuss. If this is his first ever journey, the precautions that apply to travelling any youngster are absolutely essential. Both handler and driver must be experienced and unflappable and the vehicle must be well padded, with plenty of bedding on the floor.

If possible, bring him home in a horsebox rather than a trailer. It is usually easier to give a better ride in a lorry, and it is also easier to hear if anything is going wrong. If necessary, hire a good professional transporter – in fact, this can be a good idea all round unless you are very experienced at handling and travelling youngsters. Take a travelling companion to collect him – choose a quiet, seasoned traveller who can be relied upon (as far as you can ever rely on horses) not to kick or bite or to get upset. You should also find that it will be easier to load him if he can see that there is another horse waiting in the lorry.

If you are buying a three- or four-year-old who has been backed or even started work under saddle, it is advisable to get his shoes taken off first. He will be less likely to do any damage, either to himself or the vehicle, if he gets worried during the journey. Ignore advice to ask your vet for a mild tranquilliser: this would slow the horse's reactions down and it is important that he is aware of the movement of the vehicle so that he can balance himself.

If the horse is accustomed to wearing travelling gear, use it. If not – or if he has never been stabled and you are going to turn him straight out into a field – then ignore the standard advice on travelling protection and put nothing more than a leather head-collar on him. Never travel a horse in a nylon headcollar, even an older experienced one: if anything does go wrong and the horse struggles, leather will break. Nylon might not – at least, not before the horse's neck snaps.

It takes time and patience to get a horse used to bandages, boots, rugs and all the other paraphernalia. If the horse is unshod, the vehicle well padded and the floor has a layer of bedding on it, he is unlikely to come to harm. It also means that you do not have to struggle removing boots or bandages from a youngster who is dancing around in excitement at his new surroundings.

Try and time your journey so that you arrive home in daylight, thus giving your horse the chance to get used to new surroundings. Ideally you will have prepared a stable with a deep bed, hay ready and waiting for him and no projections on which he could hurt himself when he rolls – which he will probably do quite quickly. Make sure that he can see other horses stabled nearby and try and arrange things so that he has a quiet couple of hours to settle in, without other horses being led past.

Some horses surprise you and settle straight away, while others take longer. No matter how proud you are of your new acquisition, or how keen other people on the yard are to see him, put a ban on visitors until he is calm and happy in his surroundings. Once he has had a roll and starts tucking in to his haynet, you are halfway there.

To start with, keep to his previous routine as much as possible even if you intend to change it eventually. For instance, if he has been turned out in the day and kept in at night, stick to that. If he has been fed on Bloggs' coarse mix, start on that and only make a gradual changeover to your preferred food when he is well and truly settled.

Turning out for the first time is usually enjoyable for the horse and stressful for the owner, who is worried that his or her new baby is going to slip and hurt himself, get kicked or do any of the other things horses are so good at. All you can do is minimise the risks and cross your fingers. For instance, if you buy a horse in winter, do not put a New Zealand rug on him until he has been introduced to rugs in his stable and accustomed to wearing them. If you simply try and stick a rug on and lead the horse out, he is likely to try and turn himself inside out – as too many people find out to their cost.

One school of thought advises that brushing boots should be put on lively horses when they are in the field, but sometimes this can do more harm than good. It is easy for mud and dirt to work its way between the boot and the leg, which may rub and set up skin infection. If you do decide to use boots, the horse must again be accustomed to them before you turn him out.

Never turn a horse out on his own if he is not used to it. Some yards have a policy of turning each horse out in a separate small paddock, their theory being that they are less likely to get hurt this way. In practice you run just as much – or even more – risk of injury, as often horses charge up and down or try to jump out and get to the one in the next field. It is almost a dead cert that a youngster who is turned out on his own when he has been used to companionship will panic and try and get over (or through) the fence.

The choice of companion is important. Ideally it should be a quiet animal that is unshod or at least has had its back shoes removed. It also helps if it is the same sex as your youngster. Keeping one mare and gelding together sometimes (though not always) works, but when you get a 'mixed herd' situation, as happens in some DIY livery set-ups, you are asking for trouble. Often a gelding will fall in love with a particular mare and do everything possible to prevent the other horses getting near her. It is also rather a nuisance if you happen to be that mare or filly's owner and cannot catch her because her Romeo keeps chasing her away.

Once your youngster and his companion have settled down, then you can start introducing other horses of the same sex. Inevitably there will be squabbles as they sort out the 'pecking order', and sometimes the new arrival will be kept right on the edge of the social group for a while. Eventually one horse will accept the new one (usually the one who was previously lowest in the hierarchy) and you will see them grazing together. When that happens, it is usually not long before the others accept him as well.

Feeding

Many people are so anxious that their youngsters get all the nutrients they need for growth that they go over the top and overfeed. This can cause all sorts of problems. If the immature limbs are expected to support too great a bodyweight the result can be permanent damage. The showing world in particular used to be criticised for the prevalence of fat youngstock in in-hand classes, but the message is starting to get through. There is a world of difference between the fat animal and the one who is well done, as can be seen by watching the most successful competitors.

The horse is a 'trickle' feeder by nature; if he gets the chance, he will graze for most of the time. Forage is the most important part of his diet, so it is vital that he is turned out on good grazing with equally good fencing and adequate shelter. Good does not mean too rich, and if the horse starts looking too podgy or could be at risk from laminitis it is important to move him to a barer field or to fence off part of your lush pasture as a 'diet paddock'.

Electric fencing is excellent for this and most horses soon learn to give it a wide berth. Remember that laminitis does not only strike fat little ponies: even Thoroughbreds are at risk. Youngsters winter out quite happily as long as they have enough to eat and the protection of a thick hedge or field shelter, though by all means bring him in at night if your grazing is limited or you are worried about security. Good quality hay is as important as good quality hard feed and pasture, as dust and mould spores can soon set up respiratory problems.

Every horse must be treated as an individual when working out hard feed requirements; a two-year-old native pony will have very different needs from a two-year-old Thoroughbred. Ready-formulated feeds which contain all the necessary vitamins and minerals make life much simpler for the average owner – all the reputable feed companies have their own nutritionists, who will give free advice based on their products.

If you are feeding coarse mix or nuts, you should not need to add a vitamin and mineral supplement. The only exception is if your horse or pony is such a good doer that you have to feed less than the manufacturers' recommendations. In this case, ask them whether you need to feed a broad spectrum vitamin and mineral supplement at half the recommended 'dosage'.

Your aim should always be to have your horse looking well and happy but behaving sensibly. For your sake as much as his, do not be tempted to overfeed the three- and four-year-old starting ridden work. It is far safer to back and ride horses at this stage straight from grass in the spring and summer and only to add hard feed (in small amounts to start with, until you can gauge the effect) if they need more energy.

Early handling

You may have bought a youngster who has had a good education in the basic niceties of life and is good to lead, tie up, have his feet picked out and so on. Lucky you! On the other hand, you may be faced with an ignorant, bargey animal who knows nothing – or a spoilt brat who has been fed too many titbits and learned to throw his weight about. In the last two cases, your first job is to instil some manners. It is sensible to wear gloves, boots with steel toecaps and, if necessary, a hard hat. You then have some protection if your horse decides to try and pull the rope through your hands, jump on your foot or send you flying.

When handling youngsters, there is a definite line between being firm and being aggressive. He has to accept that you are above him in the pecking order and that what you say, goes. This does not mean that you are in any way cruel to him, but it does mean that you might occasionally feel that you are running a remand school for delinquent equines!

It is also important that you handle him from both sides, right from the start. For some reason we are brainwashed into thinking that we should do everything from the nearside, which means that there are an awful lot of 'one sided' horses.

A headcollar and leadrope do not give you a lot of control over a big, pushy two- or three-year-old, and once he learns that he can walk all over you he will do just that. The remedy is simple: get his teeth checked and if necessary rasped by your vet or equine dentist and bit him with a mild bit (see Chapter 4). A coupling and leadrope will help persuade him that you are to be respected and listened to. There will be no need to be rough and as long as he is bitted correctly, there is no fear that his mouth will be damaged.

Foals should obviously be managed on a headcollar and this should also be possible with yearlings; if your yearling colt is too full of his own importance for your liking, ask your vet if he is ready to geld. You can give yourself more control by clipping the leadrope to the opposite side of the headcollar, then passing it under the chin and through the ring on the side nearest you. It will act like a curb chain – but it is important to ensure that the smooth side of the clip is next to the horse's jaw and the clip opening away from it, so there is no danger of it digging in to his face. If the horse is particularly big and strong or you are small and light, you can use the same technique with a Newmarket lead rein; this is a leather lead rein with a chain section at the end near the clip. Alternatively, the leadrope or chain can be passed through the side ring of the headcollar, over the nose and through the opposite side ring before being clipped to the top ring on that side.

Most horses are taught to lead as foals, but it is important from the safety point of view that your horse leads calmly and correctly. He should walk freely at your side, halting and turning as you wish, without pulling or dragging his heels. If you teach him right from the start to move off and halt from the voice, it will make life easier later on.

Equip your pushy youngster and yourself as above. Tell him to 'Walk on', and if he tries to shoot off, use your voice sharply to tell him 'No!' and give a sharp tug on the leadrope. It is important that there is a distinct give and take – a dead pull just gives him something to pull against. When he responds (and he will probably be so astonished that he comes back to you straight away) praise him and make a fuss of him. Do not use titbits to reward a youngster, as you will only encourage him to nip and threaten. The lesson will not sink in overnight, but by repeating it consistently you should soon see a big improvement.

This kind of horse is often pushy in the stable, too – and being flattened by something which tries to barge its way out as soon as you open the door is no fun. Carry a short stick when you approach and if the horse barges at you, say 'No!' sharply and hit the door. He will usually either shoot back in horror at the noise or stand still in surprise, but praise him in either case.

If hitting the door has no effect, you will have to take things a stage farther. Keeping your short stick in one hand, open the door with the other – making sure that you stand to one side as you do so. It the horse tries to barge out, reprimand him as before and hit him once across the chest. Again, he will shoot back or stop in his tracks, so praise him. As with all lessons, this will need to be repeated a few times until the message sinks in.

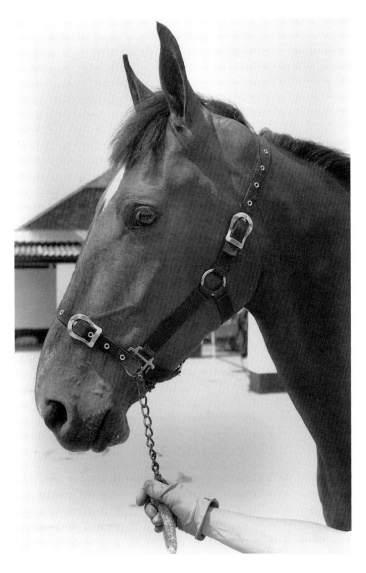

If the horse has not been bitted and you need more control than an ordinary headcollar and rope will give you, use a lead rein or rope with a chain section.

The opposite side of the coin is the horse who refuses to walk out and wants to slouch along behind you, dragging his toes and occasionally setting them firmly on the ground because he does not want to go anywhere, thank you. Equip yourself with a long schooling whip, which should be held in your outside hand, and try and find a safe leading area alongside a wall, hedge or fence.

Stand at the horse's shoulder and tell him to walk on, as before. If he does not obey, or ambles off at a snail's pace, give him a sharp tap on the girth with the whip. Be ready to go with him if he shoots off in surprise, and praise him. Horses soon get wise to the fact that they get a smack if they ignore you, and it is amazing how quickly this lesson sinks in. The barrier formed by your wall or whatever is important, as it prevents the horse from swinging his quarters away from you to avoid the whip.

Tying up

It is important that the young horse learns to accept being tied up but is neither frightened by it, nor gets the chance to learn that all he has to do to get free is pull back and break the string between the tying-up ring and his leadrope. (Tying a horse direct to a fixed ring is a surefire way to an injured horse, a demolished wall or building, or both.)

If you have a stall available, you have a headstart. Many people are horrified at the idea of putting horses in stalls, but horses themselves settle very happily as long as they have neighbours in the adjacent ones. The horse who weaves in a loose box will often relax and stop the habit altogether when stood in a stall. He must be kept on a log and rope rather than being tied up so that he can lay down and get up comfortably.

The log and rope get him used to the idea of being restrained without suddenly presenting him with the immovable object. Fasten a chain behind the horse, rather like the breeching bars in a trailer, so that if he tries to step back they come into contact with his back end. As soon as he feels the contact he will step forward, the headcollar rope will slacken and he has rewarded himself.

If you cannot use a stall, pass a lunge line through a metal tying-up ring and clip it to his headcollar. Stand at his shoulder and encourage him forwards if he tries to go back – do not stand in front of him looking back, which is likely to make him go into reverse. This method allows you to give and take without getting into a tugging match. Keep the sessions short; he will soon realise that being tied up is not so bad after all. When you are able to graduate to tying him up in the ordinary way, keep the sessions short and sweet again and do not leave him tied up unattended.

Picking up feet

The sooner a horse learns to pick up its feet when asked, the better; this is something that foals can be taught as soon as they are used to being handled. The technique is the same whether you are dealing with a foal or a three-year-old: the difference is that the bigger the horse, the more weight he has to argue with!

Start by getting him used to you running your hands over his legs. Talk to him before you touch him and start at the shoulders or quarters. Run your hands gently but firmly down over his limbs until he is used to them being handled, then give a suitable command – such as 'Up' – as you make an upward squeeze and release action just above the fetlock to ask him to lift up that leg.

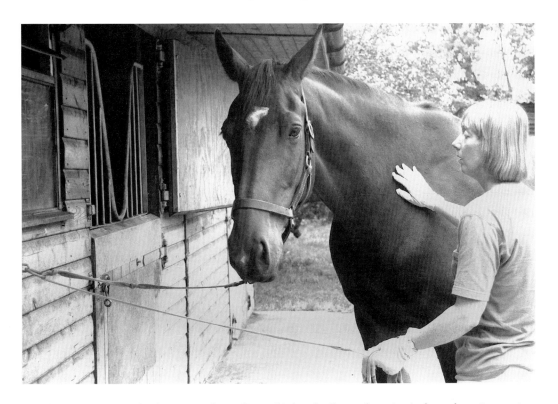

Teach a horse to tie up by fastening a lunge line to his headcollar and passing it through a tying up ring.

It is important to make sure that the horse is standing square and balanced before you attempt to pick up a foot. If his legs are all over the place, asking him to stand on three of them will put him even more off balance. He is bound to start hopping around and may even fall over, and if he associates having his feet picked up with being uncomfortable or frightened you have a real problem to contend with.

Some horses will lift their feet if you squeeze just above the fetlock, as explained above. Others seem to have the knack of transferring most of their bodyweight to the leg you want them to pick up. If, as is often suggested, you lean into their shoulders or quarters a little to persuade them to shift, they simply lean back at you – and there are no prizes for guessing who wins.

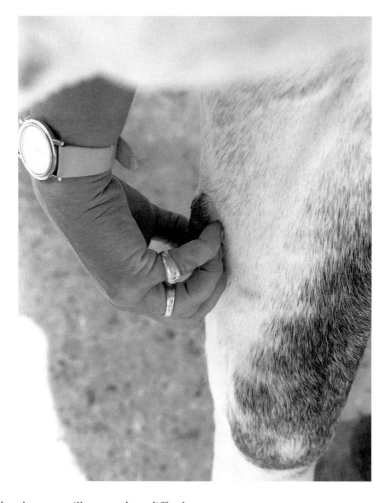

Squeezing the chestnut will persuade a difficult customer to . . . .

Rather than be the loser in a game of push and shove, run your hands down his leg with one hand and squeeze the chestnut with the other. The reaction to this can be quite sharp and quick, so make sure there is no danger of being kneed in the face. As soon as the limb comes up, let go of the chestnut and hold the foot at the toe, praising the horse.

Do not expect too much, too soon. Only ask the horse to hold his foot a little way off the ground and only ask him to hold it up for a second or two. If he struggles, try and move with him so that you keep hold of the foot, but there is no danger of him slipping and falling over, then let go when he stops fighting. If you have any doubts about your ability to cope, ask your farrier to show you how to handle the youngster. Most farriers would rather help teach a horse in the first place than be asked to sort out someone else's mistakes.

. . . . pick up his feet.

Punishment

Inevitably, there will be times when you have to punish a horse. Punishment must always be immediate – and appropriate – so that the horse learns that whatever he has done is not considered acceptable behaviour. Sometimes a sharp 'No!' or a tug on a headcollar rope is enough; sometimes you will have to hit a horse. Ninety-nine times out of a hundred, a single sharp smack on the girth with a stick is appropriate and sufficient if a horse has to be hit.

Horses are rarely aggressive, but if they do decide to show irritation or try and boss you around it is inevitably by biting or kicking. Thin-skinned horses, which means Thoroughbreds or horses with a high percentage of Thoroughbred blood, sometimes dislike being groomed or having rugs changed. Tie the horse up short enough to prevent it swinging its head round and be as considerate as you can – use a soft bristled brush or your hand rather than a stiff dandy brush, for instance. Being considerate is your part of the bargain; showing reasonable manners is the horse's, so insist that he behaves.

The old grooms used to say that the best way to punish a horse was to reply in kind. If it bit you, you got hold of its ear and bit it back; if it kicked, you put the toe of your boot in its belly. The only drawback is that you have to know exactly what you are doing to prevent injury to the horse or you . . . biting one on the ear can be a quick way of losing all your teeth.

If a horse bites you as a 'one-off', give it a sharp slap on the nose and tell it off. If biting is a habit, you need to try another tactic, as constant smacks on the nose lead to the horse becoming headshy. All that happens is that the horse bites and throws its head up or jumps out of the way to avoid being hit.

Instead, hold a metal curry comb or wear one of the dog grooming mitts with wire 'bristles'. Hold it so that as the horse swings round to bite you, his muzzle comes into contact with the business end rather than you. It will usually take only two or three goes before he decides that biting is more uncomfortable for him than for you.

Any horse will lash out in fright, but there is a big difference between the horse that kicks because it is frightened and the horse that kicks in temper. If you know a horse is thin-skinned, be careful in general and extra careful when dealing with ticklish areas such as the belly. The biggest danger here is from the horse that cow kicks, and with a ticklish horse this can be a reflex action. Wearing a hard hat or skull cap can often be a sensible precaution.

Again, the horse must offer good manners in return for your considerate handling. If he persists in kicking, tell him off and hit him with a stick on the girth. With some horses, the surprise factor of putting your knee in the belly works wonders. What you are doing is replying in kind, as horses do in the herd.

Insist on good behaviour right from the start. Too many people make the mistake of saying 'But he's only a baby, you have to make allowances' – and find themselves making allowances for a bad mannered six-year-old.

Chapter 3
New Experiences

By the time your horse reaches the yearling stage he will hopefully have learned the basics – leading, tying up, having his feet picked up and trimmed and so on. Some people then like to show their youngsters as much of life as possible, whilst others prefer to leave them to grow up relatively undisturbed until they are three and ready to back. Both approaches have their advantages and disadvantages and both can be overdone; steering a middle course can often offer the best of both worlds.

All young animals (including children!) respond to stimulation but have short attention spans. Your young horse needs time to be just that: a maturing animal who is given time to grow, play and rest. Any lessons must be short and sweet and he must be given plenty of time to get used to and recover from new experiences. By all means have a bit of fun showing him in hand, but make sure he does not become tired and jaded by the whole thing. This happens far too often on the county show circuit, when a star in-hand three-year-old vanishes into thin air instead of going on to similar success under saddle.

If you have only been used to dealing with older horses until now, it becomes quite an eye-opener to see how young horses have to learn to cope with new experiences. Everyday things like having rugs and bandages put on can be frightening if they are done carelessly, so think before you introduce something new. Horses are not stupid, but their automatic reaction to something they are not sure about is to retreat – and if they are frightened, to get the hell out of it as quickly as they can!

Common sense is vital with all horses, but even more so with youngsters. Remember to talk to him before you approach him or touch him, to warn him that something is going to happen. Get him used to being handled and groomed all over, then progress to rubbing him down with a towel. As his confidence grows, start to move the towel about more, so that eventually you can move it against him and put it over his back as if it was a numnah.

Get him used to crackling plastic bags. Tie him up in his stable and start by putting bits of carrot in a plastic bag.This is one of the rare occasions when giving titbits is recommended – horses who are always looking for treats soon learn how to nip. Keep the bag still and quiet at first, then start to rattle it a little when he associates it with food. Once he is confident, give him a titbit with one hand and touch him on the shoulder with the bag on the other.

This may sound rather peculiar behaviour, and not the sort of thing you want the neighbours to see you doing, but you are teaching your horse to trust you and accept things you introduce him to. It means that when you come to putting a saddle on him, tightening a girth and so on, he will be less likely to take fright because he has built up his own collection of experiences.

Getting out and about, in moderation, can help add to that collection. Showing for fun (as opposed to showing in deadly seriousness) can help get your horse or pony used to the hustle and bustle he will have to cope with later on. He will also have to learn to be trimmed and plaited, to behave himself in company and to travel in a horsebox or trailer. It does not matter whether or not he wins a rosette, because unless you are a professional show producer he should be there just for the experience.

A straw bale barrier makes pulling tails safer and is far better than trying to pull a tail over the stable door.

Pick a nice hot day to start the tidying up process, when he is feeling relaxed and even a little bit dozy. You will need to thin and shorten his mane, enough to plait it and to shorten and perhaps pull his tail, depending on your preferences. Once he accepts you combing through his mane, pull out a very few hairs at a time. If he is going to resent this, it will probably be when you are working near his ears, so start about halfway up and work down to the withers until he gets used to the process. Once the mane is thin enough to plait, use an old clipper blade to shorten it without getting that awful 'cut' look that is inevitable with scissors.

Do not try and pull a mane or tail all in one go. Spread it over several days, so you can stop before he gets bored or irritated and thus avoid a confrontation. Think hard before you start pulling a tail. Once done, it will need regular attention and bandaging if it is not to end up looking like a worn-out loo brush . . . so if you only intend to go to two or three shows, plaiting could be a better option.

If you do decide to pull your horse's tail, it helps if he is used to being in a stable. Get someone to hold him and talk to him while you work, and stand him in front of a barrier made from four straw bales. Stand behind the bales and slightly to one side and use your pulling comb to tweak out a few hairs at a time. If he kicks, the bales rather than you or the stable door will take the force of the blow. This method is a sensible one to use with older horses, too, and is much safer than the traditional advice of pulling a tail over the stable door. Again, the process should be carried out over several days.

Give your horse every chance to be reasonable about this sort of attention, because patience now will repay dividends later. Always remember, though, that your safety must come first: if the horse decides to be a thug and try and knock you over or squash you against the stable door, use a humane twitch and be just as careful about working in short bursts.

A humane twitch looks a bit like a large pair of nutcrackers and is fastened on the horse's top lip. Ignore anyone who tells you that it is cruel and that your horse is only behaving because he is in agony: it has now been proven that the pressure it exerts on the lip stimulates the production of natural relaxants in the body called endorphins, which explains why some horses actually become sleepy.

Other simple but effective smartening-up techniques can be done with scissors or clippers. Start by shortening the tail so that it comes to four inches (10cm) below the point of the hocks when the horse is moving, then trim excess hair from the fetlocks and inside the ears. If you close the ear gently in your hand you can trim off the excess hair poking out round the edges and still leave plenty inside for protection against flies, etc.

Once they get used to the noise and vibration, most horses accept clippers without too much trouble. Battery clippers are usually quieter than electric ones, and if you can afford it, a small, quiet pair designed for trimming rather than a full clip is a good investment. Let your youngster watch while an older, well behaved horse is trimmed up, so that he realises that there is nothing to be frightened of, then get someone to hold him and talk to him whilst you stand at his side and switch the clippers on and off several times.

Next step is to get him used to the vibration. Switch on the clippers and put your other hand on the horse's shoulder. Once he is relaxed, rest the clippers on your hand so that the vibration is muted; if he jumps or seems uneasy, keep calm, let him settle and try again until he accepts this new feeling and remains settled while the clippers are swiched on and off. Finally, rest the clippers on his shoulder. Eventually he will become blase about the whole business and you can start trimming.

Some horses always hate having clippers near their ears, no matter how careful you are. The alternatives are to leave them hairy, trim them with a small pair of scissors or use a twitch. Again, some people will throw up their hands in horror at the thought of putting a twitch on a young horse, but if it helps avoid an argument, it cannot do any harm.

Rugs and travelling equipment

If your youngster is anything but a thin-skinned Thoroughbred or nearly Thoroughbred, he will winter out quite happily in all but the most severe weather providing he has sufficient food and good shelter. This may horrify those who like to get out their New Zealands at the first sign of cold, but the fact remains that the horse's coat is the best form of insulation he could have.

Horses are quite happy in colder temperatures than most owners think. What they do not like is wind and rain, so they must be given protection from both by thick hedging and/or a field shelter. If you provide a field shelter and the horses stand at the side of it rather than going inside it, the design or siting is probably at fault. Perhaps the horses cannot get away from the prevailing winds, or maybe the entrance is too narrow or low. Horses are reluctant to go into places when they do not have a clear view of what lies ahead, and if the entrance is only wide enough to admit one horse at a time then a timid youngster will often stay outside rather than be bullied or trapped inside.

The biggest problems are caused by a combination of wind and rain, which all horses hate, and prolonged periods of heavy rain which leave the coat saturated. The horse then finds it more difficult to maintain his body temperature and is also susceptible to rain scald, a skin condition which starts up when the wide, flat areas of the back and quarters are continually wet. The only way to keep him warm and dry is to use a good New Zealand; just to prove that youngsters are as expensive to keep as mature horses, you will need two so that you have a spare when one has to be dried off.

The price of top quality rugs has gone sky high, especially the state of the art, lightweight and breathable turnout designs. Somehow the price tags look even worse when you take into account the fact that it may be too small for the horse next year . . . but think twice before buying a cheap but heavy and not very well cut rug for a youngster who is out for all or most of the time. Rugs which press on the withers or back can do as much damage as an ill-fitting saddle, especially if they are held in place by ordinary (as opposed to cross) surcingles.

Young horses are energetic and a cheap rug which is not shaped at the shoulder and quarters will rub or slip. Unfortunately the cheapest does not always work out that way in the long run: you may well find that you get a better return for your money by opting for a better quality rug in the first place and selling it secondhand when it is outgrown. If you are really lucky, you might even find a good secondhand one to start with.

Introduce rugs with care, as even the quietest youngster may take fright at this strange thing which is suddenly attached to him. Legstraps are the worst offenders – too many people fall into the trap of trying on a New Zealand in the stable and leading the horse straight out because he seems happy. They then see their quiet horse explode or

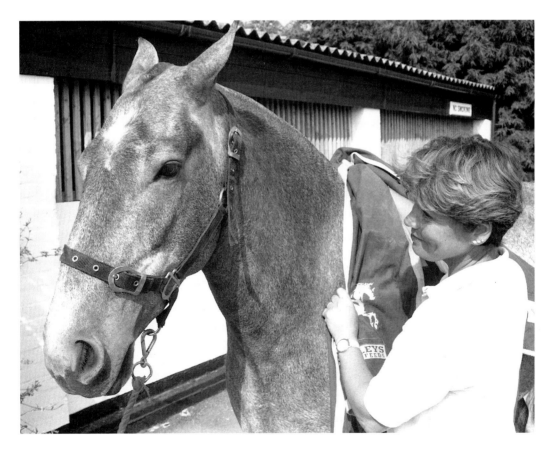

This young cob is being introduced to wearing a rug. Follow the sequence on pages 40 and 41 and keep your movements calm but confident.

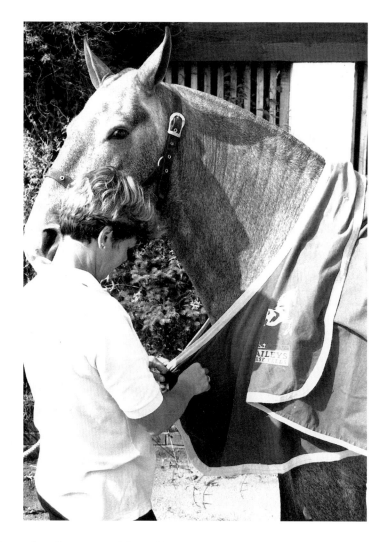

disappear into the distance at fifty miles an hour when the straps move against his legs for the first time!

Start in the stable with an old medium weight stable rug, preferably with elasticated cross surcingles, that is easy to handle. Give the horse a feed or a haynet so that he has something enjoyable to think about and either tie him up or get someone to hold him. If you have an assistant, he or she should stand on the same side as you – a horse moves away from something that frightens it. Fold the rug in half, front to back, and let him sniff it if he wants to. Place it quietly over his shoulders and fasten up the front, then unfold it along his back. Keep your movements quiet but firm and keep talking to him: if you touch him as if he is an unexploded bomb, he will probably turn into one.

He may turn round and sniff the rug, or even get hold of it in his teeth (which is a good reason for using an old one). Do up the cross surcingles equally calmly, just tight

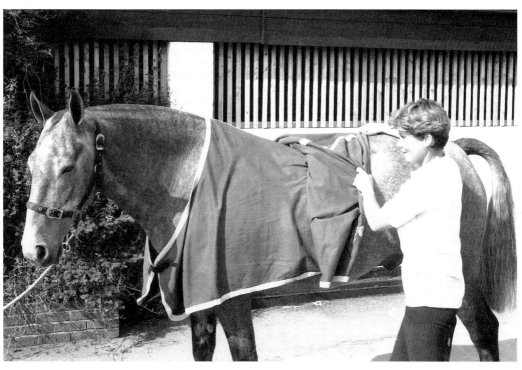

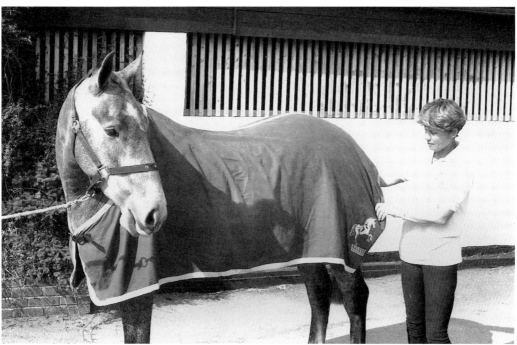

enough to hold the rug in place. If the cross surcingles are not elasticated, take them off altogether and fasten the rug with an elastic surcingle which will 'breathe' with the horse – it is not the feel of something round their belly that they dislike so much as the restriction when they breathe out and the surcingle does not.

Leave the horse for half an hour or so, keeping an eye on him to make sure he is happy, then remove the rug with as much care as you put it on. Undo the front first, then the surcingles, then fold the back to the front and slide it over his shoulder. The reason for undoing the front first is that if he moves or jumps forward when the surcingles are unfastened, the rug will not be trapped round his neck and shoulder if it starts to slide off. Trying to take off a rug that is hanging round the neck and trapped between the forelegs of a panicking horse is not a lot of fun for either of you.

Once he accepts the rug and you can lead him round the stable with him staying relaxed, you can introduce leg straps if necessary. Stand a little way out and to the side as you fasten the legstraps and move him forwards or over a step so he feels them against him. Once he moves around happily in his box with the rug in place, you can turn him out with it on.

He will also need to get used to wearing travelling equipment in preparation for the day when he goes to his first show – or, of course, if you have to travel him to the vet or farrier. Practise this at home so he has plenty of time to get used to all the paraphernalia; most horses find wearing boots or bandages very confusing and take greatly exaggerated steps until they learn to ignore them.

Horses have to learn how to keep their balance whilst travelling, and may sit back on their tails to start with. It is important to protect the dock by putting on at least a tail bandage and preferably a tailguard as well. Get your youngster accustomed to wearing a tail bandage before you try and put boots or bandages on his back legs. If you start with the tail bandage, he will get used to you working at his back end, but if you go straight to putting on leg protectors he will be more likely to lash out in fright.

Whether you use boots or bandages on the legs is down to personal choice. Boots are quicker to put on and take off, but unless they are very well designed (with a price tag to match) tend to slip. Bandages stay in place better – a lot of people worry about putting them on too tightly, but as long as you use them over suitable padding there is very little risk of this.

Most travelling boots fasten with Velcro, which is quick and easy. For this reason, it is best to use bandages with Velcro fastenings rather than tie tapes. The one disadvantage of Velcro is that it is noisy, so stand near the horse and fasten and unfasten the straps several times before you put the boots or bandages on for the first time.

If you have both available, put boots on him at home for the first few times until he gets used to his legs being encased. Walk him round in them, but do not leave him in the stable with them on or he may well decide to remove them with his teeth. Seeing your expensive travelling boots lying in shreds on the stable floor is not recommended for the sake of either your bank balance or your blood pressure.

Once he accepts them, switch to bandages. As long as they are put on correctly and fastened securely, you can leave them on the horse and lead him round in them when he first comes off the lorry. They will protect him if he knocks himself in excitement, and you do not have to take them off until he settles down.

Some people like to use knee and hock boots, but to be quite honest these can cause more trouble than they are worth. The top straps have to be fastened tightly to prevent them slipping, which is likely to make a youngster kick out in surprise, and even then they tend to shift on the leg. It is far better to protect the joints by using shaped bandage padding which extends over the knees and hocks.

Loading

Once your young horse treats rugs and travelling equipment with aplomb, you can teach him to load into a vehicle. The best way to do this is with the help of a reliable schoolmaster, so if you do not own one, try and borrow a quiet horse or pony who can be relied upon to load first time and to go in and out several times without hesitating.

The vehicle should be light, airy and if possible familiar. Try and avoid ones that are rear-unload only to start with, as it is much easier if the horse can walk straight through. Backing down a ramp when he has just gone up it for the first time is asking a bit much.

#A well-known professional horse transporter who travels bloodstock worth millions of pounds says he taught a Thoroughbred filly to load by accident: a trailer was parked in her field with the front and rear ramps down and a haynet tied up, and she got so used to it that she treated it like a field shelter, walking in and out of her own accord.

Unfortunately most of us cannot try this approach, if only because the trailer would probably be damaged, stolen or both. It does show, though, that familiarity breeds contempt – so if you can let your youngster see vehicles round the yard and watch other horses being loaded and unloaded, so much the better. When his turn comes, try and park the box or trailer alongside a wall or fence so that there is a barrier alongside and make sure that the interior is light and bright so that he can see where he is going.

Put on his travelling equipment and if he has been bitted (see Chapter 4) put his bridle, minus noseband, over the headcollar. Thread a lunge line though the nearside bit ring, under the chin and clip it to the offside ring. This gives much more control and you can then lead him up to the ramp, close behind his schoolmaster. An assistant should be on hand in case you get any problems, but should not chase the horse up the ramp. Many youngsters will happily go straight up; others will put a foot on it and hesitate. With the second scenario, do not try and hustle the horse. What he is doing is testing that the unfamiliar footing is secure, so keep calm, keep him facing forwards and ask him to walk on when he has had a chance to work it all out.

Once he is in, make a fuss of him and give him a titbit. Let him stand for a minute or two, no longer, then walk him out as carefully as you walked him in. Again, he may test the footing before coming down – and he may also take a flying leap from halfway up the ramp, hence the lunge line rather than a lead rope.

Repeat the experience and leave it at that for the first time. Over the next few days, get him used to going up the ramp and being tied up in the vehicle; make sure there is a haynet in there or time your session so that you can give him his normal feed in the vehicle. When he is standing happily, get a helper or two to fasten the breeching straps (if he is in a trailer) and close the rear ramp. His companion should give him the confidence that this is nothing to worry about, but make sure you do not stand where there is a risk of getting jumped on.

His first journey should last about 15 to 20 minutes, long enough to get him used to the sensation but not so long that he gets overtired or impatient. When you get home, give him a reward of titbits or a small feed and turn him out so he can have a roll and unwind.

Bad loaders and travellers are usually made that way by inconsiderate drivers and handlers. They can often be cured, as will be shown later in this book, but it is a lot easier to avoid problems than to solve them.

Chapter 4
Introducing Tack

Sooner or later you will get to the stage where you want to get your horse used to wearing a bit. If he tends to be on the bumptious side, make it sooner. Being dragged around on a headcollar by a horse doing an impression of a steam roller is dangerous for you and for other people. The relationship between you and your horse is a partnership, but there are times when one of you has to be boss – and it must always be you.

It is vital that you get the horse's mouth and teeth checked and any problems sorted out before you introduce a bit. If he associates wearing a bit with discomfort, perhaps because of sharp edges to his molars or because he has wolf teeth, you are setting up problems that can be difficult to cure. For instance, the horse who learns how to put his tongue over the bit will often continue to try and do so even when his teeth have been sorted out.

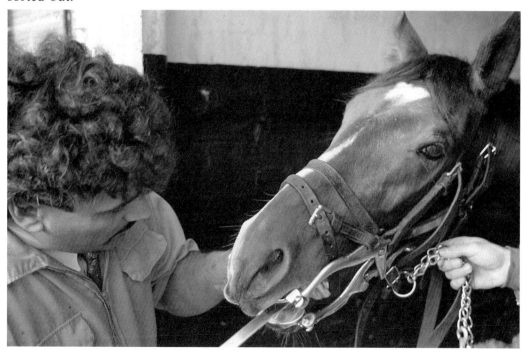

All horses should have their mouths and teeth checked regularly. It is vital that this is done before a youngster is bitted for the first time.

A horse will shed 24 teeth between the ages of two and a half and five years, so is going through the period of greatest change whilst he is learning the important basics of his education. Routine care should start when the youngster is a yearling and the horse should be checked by your vet or horse dentist twice a year for the next four years. After that he may be all right with an annual check, though some horses still need seeing twice a year.

The commonest dental problem is sharp edges on the molars, which are almost inevitable when you take into account mouth conformation and the way the horse eats. The upper molars are set slightly wider than the lower ones, and the horse chews in a round and round, grinding motion – so the inside edges of the upper molars and outer edges of the lower ones wear faster than the rest of the top surface. The resulting sharp edges, or hooks, can lead to mouth sores, poor digestion and resulting loss of condition and injuries to the gum and tongue. If the hooks are filed, or 'floated', the discomfort will be eased.

Wolf teeth are another common cause of trouble. These are very small, shallow-rooted teeth which erupt in front of the premolars – usually in the upper jaw, but occasionally also in the lower one. They are in just the right place to get knocked by the bit, which is painful for the horse and not surprisingly sets up a chain reaction of resistance.

There are two schools of thought on wolf teeth. One says that they should be left alone unless they cause trouble, the other that they are of no use anyway and should be removed as a matter of course. As their removal is quick and easy when carried out by a skilled practitioner, it makes sense to have them taken out – you get enough unavoidable problems with young horses, so why not eliminate the avoidable ones?

A lot of people confuse wolf teeth with tushes. Tushes, or canine teeth, are present in male horses (and very occasionally in mares, too). They erupt at between four and five years and though the horse may be uncomfortable whilst they are coming through, they rarely cause any problems once they are settled.

One of the authors bought a Thoroughbred mare out of a racing yard who stuck her head in the air, opened her mouth and did an excellent impression of a giraffe. Her previous owner's advice was to 'put a running martingale on' – but when she was examined by a leading equine dentist, he found that she had wolf teeth. Once these were taken out and she realised that contact on the reins did not mean pain, she settled and went on to become a lovely ride. The same dentist was called in to look at another mare who evented and show jumped successfully but was known as a 'difficult ride'. She too had wolf teeth, and she too became a much more relaxed ride when they were removed. Amazingly, this mare was ten years old before anyone thought to see if there was a physical cause for what had been dismissed as 'marish' behaviour!

Once you know that your horse is as comfortable as possible in his mouth, you can introduce a bit. Again, there are all sorts of theories as to which bit is the best to start with and all have their pros and cons. Bitting is a fascinating and controversial subject. For now, you have to accept that whatever bit you choose, the horse may start by trying to spit it out: after all, what would you do if someone suddenly put a piece of metal or rubber in your mouth?

A loose-ring, hollow mouthed snaffle is often a good one to start with – the loose rings allow some play and the lightweight mouthpiece is often more acceptable to the horse than a heavier one in the earlier stages. The important points are that the bit must be the correct width, reasonably thick but not so thick that the horse cannot close his mouth round it comfortably and adjusted high enough to prevent him getting his tongue over it.

A breaking bit with keys to encourage the horse to 'mouth'.

Some horses respond much better if you start them off with an old-fashioned mouthing bit with keys on it. The keys encourage the horse to play with the mouth-piece and to relax his jaw, rather than setting it against this 'foreign object' that has suddenly been put in his mouth. You can achieve the same effect by holding the ends and flylink of a short double-link curb chain together and fastening it to the centre of the bit. However, if the horse is fussy in his mouth, anything that encourages him to play may make the situation worse, so in this situation you will be better off with an ordinary bit.

When it comes to choosing the right size, you have a Catch 22 situation in that you do not know what this is until you have actually fitted it. Big horses do not always have wide mouths, and vice versa: it is quite possible for a 16.2hh horse to need a five inch mouthpiece and a 14.2hh pony to need a five and a half inch one. The only answer is a combination of instinct and inspired guesswork: unless you are breaking a small pony or a Thoroughbred with a narrow muzzle, try a five and a half inch to start with.

Many horses object not so much to holding a bit in their mouth as to having their ears put through the gap between browband and headpiece. Get your horse used to having the headpiece put on without a bit first, to avoid the risk of him taking the bit calmly but throwing up his head – and banging himself in the teeth – when the bridle goes over his ears. Make sure that the browband is wide enough not to pinch the base of his ears: it might sound obvious, but it is something a lot of people forget to check and then wonder why their horses shake their heads.

For simplicity's sake, leave off the noseband to start with. The less you have to cope with while you are persuading the horse to open his mouth, the better. At this stage you can also make a rough guess at the correct adjustment for the cheekpieces, bearing in mind that you will want the bit to wrinkle the corners of the horse's mouth. Leave the straps out of the keepers, so that you can adjust them quickly if necessary.

Coat the mouthpiece of the bit in molasses or honey before you fit it for the first time; if it tastes nice, the horse will be more inclined to accept it. All you have to do then is persuade him to open his mouth! The standard technique of pressing on the bars with your thumb is often enough of an irritant to make him open up long enough to slip the mouthpiece in; if this fails, try tickling his tongue. If his mouth stays obstinately shut, rub molasses or honey inside his lips – you will probably get a lot messier than he does, but you should be able to slide the bit in as he investigates the taste.

Your movements should be gentle but quick. Once the bit is in place, make any adjustments necessary and fasten the throatlatch. The bit should be wide enough to allow *no more* than a half inch gap on each side between the cheekpieces and the horse's lips: if it is any wider, the bit will hang too low in the horse's mouth and encourage him to put his tongue over. It will also bang on his teeth and the sides of his mouth. A mouthpiece which is too narrow will also be uncomfortable for him, as it will pinch. A straight-sided bit which stays still in the mouth, such as an eggbutt, full cheek or D-ring can fit slightly more snugly than a loose ring.

Bits are made in increments of about half an inch, but unfortunately horses' mouths do not always follow the same scale. If yours is between sizes, go for the larger rather than the smaller and adjust it a hole higher. Some manufacturers have stuck to the traditional imperial measurement system, but others have gone metric – which gives more scope to find a bit that fits. If you cannot get a good fit with a metric sized bit, try an old-fashioned imperial one, and vice versa.

At first glance, these bits (above and overleaf) may look as if they are fitted in a similar way, but in the second picture the mouthpiece is slightly too low. The first picture shows the correct adjustment; if the horse tries to put his tongue over the bit, it could be fastened a hole higher.

Your horse needs to get used to the feel of a bit, but you should not leave it in so long for the first time that he resents it. Fifteen minutes is usually enough for a first attempt; make sure there is nothing in the stable for him to get the bit caught up on, and stay with him. Remove the bridle with as much care as you put it on, as if the bit bangs on his teeth – or even worse, gets caught up – he will be very wary next time round.

Some horses accept a bit straight away, but others take longer. If yours is convinced that he can spit it out if he keeps trying, let him wear it whilst you lead him around. Use

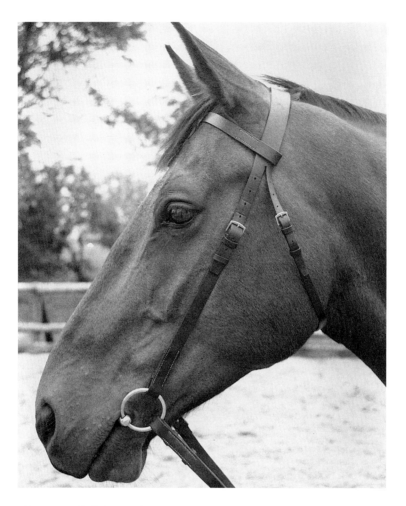

Here the mouthpiece is slightly too low.

a bridle without a noseband and fit it over a headcollar so there is no interference with the bit. (You may have to lower the bit by a hole to allow for the bulk of the headcollar underneath the cheekpieces.) Fasten a lunge line to the headcollar and let the horse pick at some grass with his bit in. You can also leave him standing in the stable for short periods, but make sure that there is nothing that the bit rings could get hooked up on.

You can now introduce a saddle or roller. If the horse has been used to wearing rugs, he will be halfway towards accepting things on his back and round his belly; if not, start by getting him used to an elastic surcingle. It does not matter whether you use a roller or a saddle, but you do not want to risk an expensive saddle getting damaged. Some people like to use a lightweight synthetic or racing saddle to start with, whilst others start as they mean to go on and use an old leather one.

Whatever you use, it is important to pay attention to fit. Too many people use any old roller, but ones which press on the withers or do not have enough clearance either side of the spine can do just as much damage as badly fitting saddles. A foam pad underneath gives extra protection, and many trainers like to use a breastgirth for added security; this means there is no risk of the roller sliding back and encouraging the horse to buck.

The saddle you use must clear the withers, have a wide enough gullet to prevent the risk of pressure on the spinous processes and have wide enough panels to give a large weight distribution area. It must also sit correctly behind the shoulders so that the flaps do not interfere with the horse's movement. Getting a good fit on a young horse who is higher at the back than the front is sometimes easier said than done, but use your common sense at this stage and be very careful about the fit of a saddle when you start ridden work.

If you are using a leather saddle, a thin numnah will reduce the shock of cold leather on the horse's back. Make sure it is pulled up into the gullet so it does not pull down on the withers. The advantage of synthetic saddles is that they are lightweight and warm (and cheap!); the disadvantage is that not all makes are well designed.

Let the horse sniff the saddle or roller (and if you are using a saddle, remove the irons and leathers before putting it on. You do not need them to start with and if they come down and bang against the horse's side he will probably take fright.) Once he seems happy with this strange object, slide it gently into position whilst an assistant makes a fuss of the horse. If you are using a roller, be careful that the ends do not bang down against the horse's sides.

The horse may lift his head to look at the strange object that has appeared on his back and perhaps step forwards or sideways round the stable. Hold the saddle or roller in place and move with him, talking to him all the time. As with all stages of training, some horses will be wary of this new experience and some will accept it without turning a hair. The important thing is that the saddle does not fall off and frighten him, so slide it off and start again rather than risk this happening.

Once he is relaxed, get your assistant to pass the end of the girth or roller down the side and underneath the horse's belly. He or she should move to stand on the same side as you before you attempt to fasten it, as if the horse objects he will move away from you, not towards you and may squash your helper. Hold it round his belly, fasten it just tightly enough to keep everything in place, and get out of the way.

With luck, the horse will stay calm. However, you get the odd one who reacts violently when he moves forward and feels the restriction round his belly. If he is going to kick or perform a rodeo in his stable, you want to be well out of the way. As long as the girth is fastened tight enough to keep the saddle in place, he will soon settle.

Once he accepts his new tack, you can introduce side reins to get him used to contact through the bit. These must be long enough at first so that he only has the weight of the rein to cope with, and should preferably have elastic or rubber inserts which allow a certain amount of 'give'. Side reins introduce the concept which the rider's hands later take over. For this reason, they must be fitted high up, not halfway down the girth, and it is important that they are not too short. You want the horse to be comfortable with the rein, not be pulled in by it.

Side reins adjusted correctly so that there is a light contact when the horse's nose is on the vertical.

It has to be said that some people hate side reins and never use them, because they feel that they are too restricting. If adjusted too short, they can do more harm than good – but as long as the horse has enough freedom of movement for his stage of training, they let him find out the barriers for himself. If he tries to throw his head about or put his nose on the floor, he will set up pressure on the bit. In the same way, he will learn that if he gives to them, the pressure will cease.

By the time you get to this stage, you will have covered a lot of ground and your horse will have learned a lot of new things. With some horses, it is all plain sailing and they are wearing their tack like old hands in a couple of days. With others, you have to persuade them that it is not as dreadful as they seem to think and the whole process takes much longer. Time scales are irrelevant, within reason: some horses simply take longer than others. Do not worry if a friend's youngster is backed and ridden away in three days whilst yours takes three weeks – as long as you make progress, it does not matter how slow it is.

Experienced trainers who are used to dealing with young horses inevitably go faster than someone making a first attempt. This is because they are used to judging horses' reactions and know when to make the next step and when to press on. In general, it is best to play safe and take your time – though no one is suggesting that you should take weeks and weeks to get your horse used to wearing a saddle and bridle! If the horse seems uneasy about a new experience, repeat it until he settles and accepts it. Only then can you go on to the next stage.

Loose schooling

Loose schooling is very useful at all stages of a horse's training, from the two- or three-year-old to the older horse being loose schooled over fences. It puts less strain than lungeing on immature limbs and joints (especially hocks) but teaches the horse to go forwards and to obey the voice.

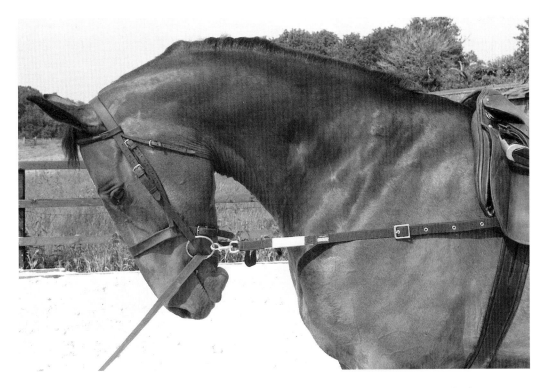

Side reins too short, which encourages the horse to overbend and come behind the bit.

Those are the advantages. The disadvantages are that you are working an exuberant young horse in an enclosed area with nothing more to influence him than your voice and body stance. As horses do not realise that they are expected to behave by the book, there is a risk that you may find yourself closer than you would like to a pair of flying hindlegs – so it is essential that you are alert and agile.

If you are working on your own, you need a confined area about 30 metres square; anything larger allows the horse to tank off and do his own thing, and if he has the chance, he probably will. Unless yours is the sort of lunatic who has no respect for any barrier, in which case loose schooling is not a good idea, you can usually work safely in a fenced-off part of your school or arena – or even the corner of a field. Your barriers must be high enough to impress; jump stands and poles do a good enough job in most cases.

The horse should wear a headcollar and protective boots and should be introduced to a lunge whip before you start. Carry it in the stable and let him get used to the sight of it, then run it along his neck, shoulders, back and quarters on both sides. If your horse is used to wearing travelling gear, brushing boots will not be very different. If not, get him used to the sound of Velcro opening and closing and remember that he may kick when he walks forwards and feels the back boots. Boots with strap and buckle fastenings are fine and even preferable for some circumstances, but are fiddly and time consuming when dealing with a youngster.

Some people like to work with just a lunge whip, whilst others prefer to carry a lunge whip in one hand as a driving aid and a schooling whip about a metre long in the other as a slowing down aid. If you decide to use both (and it really is a lot of fuss and bother) practise with an experienced horse first so that you neither frighten the horse by waving whips about when you do not mean to nor fall over the lunge whip because you are concentrating on the other one.

Lead the horse into the working area so he is near the fence, positioned to go off on the left rein (simply because most horses find working on the left rein easier than working on the right.) If he shoots off like a lunatic, let him have his fling then bring him back to walk when you can – he should know the voice commands to walk on, trot and halt already. If he stands and looks at you with a 'What on earth are we doing now?' expression, or ambles about the school, position yourself so you that if a line was drawn from you to the horse, it would end behind the girth but in front of the quarters. This is the driving position.

Encourage him to walk on and then to trot. When he settles, stand so the imaginary line drawn between you reaches to the front of his shoulder and ask him to walk and halt. Drive him forwards from behind and slow him down from in front, pointing the whip towards him and to the ground when going forwards and behind you when slowing down.

When he stops, walk up to him and make a fuss of him, then take hold of the headcollar, turn him and do exactly the same on the other rein. After a few ten-minute sessions he will get the hang of it; keep your loose schooling sessions short and sweet so he does not get bored.

Loose schooling lets you watch your horse moving naturally, without the encumbrance of a rider or the restriction of a lunge rein, and is a good way of assessing how naturally well balanced or otherwise he is. It is also the best way of introducing canter – establish an energetic trot, then give the voice command. By now he should understand that an upwards inflexion in your voice means 'Move up a gear'; it does not matter if he falls into canter and falls back into trot, as the refinements come later.

Chapter 5
Lungeing and Long Reining

Basic lungeing

Lungeing is a useful but often overrated stage in the training process. Its most important function is to reinforce the young horse's response to the voice, which is very useful when you are actually on his back and riding. If he responds to commands such as 'Walk on', 'Trot' and 'Whoa' you have a headstart in establishing communication – and when the lines of communication break down, as they inevitably will, the voice aids are a vital back-up.

One of the authors of this book took a four-year-old to its first show and was riding quietly round the showground when the horse took fright and bolted. He jumped a post and rail fence, giving proof of his jumping ability that was not exactly appreciated at the time, and was heading for a busy road oblivious of everything but his own fear. She dropped the reins completely and said 'Whoa' in the same tone that had been used when lungeing and long reining; he was so used to this and the response was so automatic that the command penetrated his fright and he came to a halt. This example might be extreme, but it is proof of the power of the voice.

Lungeing also gives a fresh horse the opportunity to let off steam. If he is going to buck and bounce around, it is better that he does it before you get on him rather than afterwards. Again, the voice commands can get through when all else fails; once he has had his fling you can ask him to put his brain back between his ears and pay attention to you. By introducing transitions – walk to trot, trot to walk and walk to halt – you can start introducing the idea of working from behind. Transitions mean the horse has to put his hindlegs underneath him to stay balanced, and it is easier for him to do this without the interference of a rider's weight.

Those are the benefits . . . but remember that unless you are a particularly skilled practitioner, lungeing is really just going round in circles. It is hardly likely to keep the horse interested, and too much can do him actual physical harm. His joints, particularly the hock joints, are being asked to take more strain than they can cope with.

A horse should not be lunged until he is three years old, and even then it should be done in moderation. He should be worked on as large an area as possible, which means that the handler must make a small circle whilst the horse describes a much bigger one – with the young horse, forget the textbook advice about standing on one spot whilst the horse makes a perfect 20-metre circle round you.

Because his movement is restricted by the length of the lunge line he will find it difficult to stay in balance at first. This means he is in danger of knocking himself, so fit brushing boots all round and, if necessary, overreach boots. The latter must be trimmed to fit; if they are so long that the horse can tread on one, trip himself up and fall flat on his face, they can cause more accidents than they prevent.

The horse should wear a headcollar or lungeing cavesson to start with. Many people use a lungeing cavesson without thinking, simply because it is the 'correct' equipment for the job, when a headcollar would make a better introduction. Some young horses hate the lunge rein at the front of their face and get the idea much better if they start off with a leather headcollar, fastened snugly enough not to slip but not so tight as to be uncomfortable, with the lunge rein clipped to the back ring as you would if you were leading the horse. Starting off with a headcollar also makes changing the rein easier, as you do not have to adjust the lunge rein: with a cavesson it tends to catch on one side ring or the other even if fastened to the centre ring unless you adjust it each time.

If the horse does not mind the lunge rein in front of his face, and you particularly want to use a lungeing cavesson, then by all means do so. The Wels cavesson fits lower on the nose than the standard pattern and gives more control – when used with a bit, the noseband acts like a drop. As with a drop noseband, care must be taken not to fit it so low that it restricts the horse's breathing (even if there are times when you think this might be a good idea!) The lunge line should be fastened to the centre ring of the cavesson.

You need an enclosed area in which to lunge a young horse. The barriers stop him wandering too far and also mean he is less tempted to try and tank off. If he does decide to disappear in the opposite direction at a great rate of knots, then a lunge rein and cavesson or headcollar do not give you much control. Lungeing a young horse in an open field is therefore a waste of time.

If you can, lunge in a fenced-in school. If not, build your own lungeing area in the corner of a reasonably level field and accept that you will have to restrict sessions to times when the going is reasonable – you do not want your young horse slipping on wet ground. Use oil drums and poles to make a circle with a diameter of about 25 metres, a sort of poor man's version of the special lungeing rings often used by racehorse trainers. The barrier must be high enough to discourage ideas of jumping out.

There are two ways of teaching a horse to lunge. The first is with the help of an assistant who walks round on the inside of the circle, staying about three feet in from the horse. He or she acts as a back-up to the trainer's voice and whip commands, encouraging the horse forwards with a schooling whip if necessary and stopping him when the trainer gives the commands.

The trouble with this approach is that the horse has to divide his attention between two people. It is much better to try and teach the horse alone so that he only has to focus on you – and easier than most people think! Kit him out in his lungeing equipment, get him used to and confident with the lunge whip as explained earlier, and start down the long side of the school or round the edge of your fenced off area.

Start on the left rein, which is the one most horses find easiest, and lead him as normal to get him used to the 'Walk on', 'Whoa' and 'Trot' commands (which he should have been taught earlier.) Remember it is the tone of voice that matters more than what you actually say: commands for upwards transitions should be brisk, with an upwards inflection, and those for downwards ones should be more drawn out and soothing. The lunge rein should be held in your left hand; never wrap the line round your hand, because if the horse takes off you could be badly hurt. Gloves are also essential.

The lunge whip should be held in your right hand, facing back and to the ground. Once he is listening and settled, allow the lunge rein out until you are about six feet apart and walking level with his shoulder. Repeat the commands as before, then change reins and try again. If you have been able to teach your horse to lead from both sides right from the start, you should not have many problems, but if you have bought a youngster who has only been led from the nearside, he may find being asked to work on the right rein a bit confusing to start with.

The lunge rein should be held at roughly your waist height and the whip can be moved forwards and down so it is pointing towards his quarters. Change the whip position quietly whilst he is standing still; some horses worry about lunge whips even if they have never been hit with one. As he gets the hang of it all, move him gradually on to a large circle if you have been working round the edge of a school. Stay about six feet away from him and walk a circle yourself: if you suddenly release the lunge line and allow him 20 metres of freedom he will either wander aimlessly around or take off in delight.

You should aim for a steady contact on the lunge rein but not a pull; if the horse leans on it, give and take until he learns that he has to balance himself. The shorter rein gives you much more control than a longer one and you will find it much easier to teach the horse what you want him to do. Aim for a slight bend to the inside of your circle, but do not pull his head in so much that his quarters fall out. Keep the sessions short, ten minutes or so to start with. As he becomes more proficient, ease out the rein until he is making the big circle and you are walking a much smaller one – but if you get problems at any time, go back to the shorter lunge rein.

The whip is an aid to impulsion and can also be used to help prevent the horse falling in on the circle. It acts as a driving aid when pointing towards his quarters and encourages him to move out on to the circle again when pointing at his shoulders. Sending a ripple down the lunge line also encourages him to move out.

Your position is important, as with loose schooling. If you stand slightly behind the girth, you are encouraging him forwards, but if you move to his shoulder, you are encouraging him to slow down. It has to be said, however, that some horses accept encouragement and some ignore it! You have to have quick reactions to lunge successfully – in fact with some horses you need reactions that are lightning sharp – because some clever souls will slow down and turn in to face you, leaving you out of control and probably feeling rather stupid. If this happens, or (even better) if you can anticipate it, step quickly back into your driving position and move the horse on.

Some horses will lunge beautifully on one rein and decide they do not want to go round on the other. Rather than have a battle, when you change to the difficult rein start off in a straight line with your short lunge rein and gradually move on to a circle as the horse is going forwards.

More advanced lungeing

In theory your horse should soon get to the stage where you can lunge him from a headcollar or cavesson. In practice you may find that he is one of those clever souls who soon works out that when you are 20 metres away from him you have little control. The only answer is to lunge him off the bit; some purists may throw up their hands in horror at this idea, but perhaps they have never been towed round a school by a youngster who has decided that he is fed up with this going-round-in-circles lark.

Never clip the lunge rein directly to the bit, as the pressure on the mouth is too direct and it is too easy for it to pull right through the horse's mouth. The simplest and mildest way is to pass the lunge rein through the bit ring nearest you, under the horse's chin like a curb chain and clip it to the other ring. If you are lungeing on the left rein, pass the lunge rein through the nearside ring and clip it to the offside one. When you change the rein, you need to alter the rein – pass it through the offside ring, under the chin and fasten it to the nearside one.

Once he accepts that you are the boss, you may be able to go back to the cavesson when you introduce side reins. (Obviously you cannot fasten side reins to a headcollar.) If not, stick with this method of lungeing from the bit. As long as you keep a light hand and make sure that the horse is working from behind, you will not get conflicting signals from the reins.

Side reins, which your horse has already worn in the stable, are used now to get him used to working up to a contact. They are not used to pull the horse's head in; if they are adjusted too short for the horse's stage of training you will simply set up resistance. It is also important that they are not attached too low, as this puts downward pressure on the bars of the mouth.

It does not matter whether you use a saddle or a roller. If you use a saddle, remove the stirrup leathers and irons or fasten them so that there is absolutely no danger of them falling down and banging against the horse's sides or elbows – a surefire way to start a rodeo. Put an overgirth on to stop the saddle flaps banging about: this too can frighten a young horse.

Start by fastening the side reins not to the bit but to the side rings of the cavesson, so the horse gets used to the idea. They should have rubber or elastic inserts to allow some give (a more sympathetic feel for a young horse than is offered by plain leather ones). Even better – if you can find them – are side reins adapted from strong rubber fastenings used in horseboxes, which have a small amount of 'give' through their entire length.

They should be fitted loosely at first, so that he has nothing more than the weight of the rein to accept. A lot of people will tell you never to lead a horse with side reins attached in case he resists or throws a buck and thus brings himself up against the rein – but as long as the reins are long enough not to interfere with his mouth at walk, where is the harm in leading him out with them already on? He might as well learn right from the start that life is much more comfortable when he gives to the rein, and that if he throws a tantrum he is only punishing himself.

Once you know that he is not worried by the reins, shorten them so that there is a very light contact when he stands with his nose on the vertical. Work in walk and trot as before, introducing gradually more frequent upward and downward transitions to encourage him to come up off his forehand. By doing this you are teaching him the basics of the half-halt, one of the most important aids to achieving balance.

Do not canter your three-year-old on the lunge yet, as cantering circles puts too much strain on immature hocks. Stick to walk and trot and keep sessions to a maximum of 20 minutes. Lungeing might look easy to you, but it is actually quite hard work for the horse: 20 minutes on the lunge is equivalent to an hour's quiet hacking.

When you attach the side reins to the bit for the first time, have them loose and floppy so that the horse has only the weight of the rein to cope with. Once he accepts them and is working happily, tighten them very gradually. Again, they should never be tighter than would give a light contact when the horse's head is on the vertical.

Most lunge work is done in walk and trot, and as the horse's outline is naturally shorter in trot than in walk, you will find that side reins adjusted 'by the book' for trot work are too restricting in walk. The usual suggestion is to keep walk work to the minimum, but you do not want to keep your horse trotting round in circles – he needs frequent rests. A more realistic approach is to keep the side reins on the long side so that you can encourage him to work forwards without the danger of restricting his walk (the easiest pace to spoil).

Some people like using side reins, whilst others are totally against them because they feel they encourage a horse to resist against a dead contact. It comes down to knowing your horse and being able to assess the way he goes: now and again you find one who has not read any books like this and either tucks his nose in to avoid the contact or sticks his head in the air and says 'Won't.'

Either get a very experienced trainer to help you, or forget the side reins and perhaps consider using a chambon. (See Chapter 12). With some horses, it is easier to teach them from the saddle, especially when you can get them hacking out. With more to interest them, they are less likely to concentrate on resisting. It cannot be stressed too strongly that lungeing has its uses, but also its limitations.

Long reining

Long reining used to be a standard part of every horse's early training, and a lot of the old grooms and nagsmen were real artists in this skill. Now it tends to be missed out and/or misunderstood, which is a pity. A lot of people think that it is difficult and are worried that they will spoil their horses' mouths, when in fact any competent handler can learn to long rein successfully.

As long as you are reasonably sensitive and confident – which are in any case both prerequisites for anyone wanting to break and train a horse – you can learn how to long rein. It is an excellent way of teaching a horse to accept the bit and to understand how to stop, start and turn without having to cope with the added complication of a rider on his back at the same time. If your horse understands rein signals to stop, start, turn left and turn right, think how much easier it will be to communicate with him when you are on his back!

It is possible for a very skilled handler to work a horse in long reins to a higher degree than most of us can achieve in the saddle. The horses of the Spanish Riding School in Vienna perform passage, piaffe and even airs above the ground in long reins. You might get these by accident, but teaching them is beyond the scope of this book! However, it is perfectly possible to obtain acceptance of the bit and the refinements of stopping, starting and steering.

You can also use long reining as a method of getting your young horse out and about. He can go round quiet roads and tracks with an older schoolmaster to get him used to all the sights and sounds he will meet later on: the wider his experience of life before you actually start riding him, the easier his first outings under saddle should be.

Long reining is less stressful than lungeing, as the horse is not working on a continuous circle. For this reason, some people like to long rein two-year-olds. If the youngster is well developed, very short sessions will not do him any harm – but they must be no longer than about 15 minutes and you must remember that new experiences are physically and mentally tiring. You have to assess your horse as an individual; if he is gangly and awkward, leave him to acquire another year's maturity, but if he is well-grown and full of his own importance, giving him something to think about may do him good.

If you have never long reined before, practice on an older horse first. It is not difficult, but manipulating two long reins and learning where to position yourself, when to give the aids to turn and so on have to be learned. If you do not know whether or not the horse has been long reined before, introduce the long reins with the same care that will be needed when you start on your youngster – even seemingly 'bomb-proof' horses have been known to explode when they suddenly feel a rein' round their quarters!

For the first attempts, start in an enclosed area. Your horse should wear a lunging cavesson, protective boots and either a roller or a saddle. If you use a roller, the long reins will go through the side rings; with a saddle, adjust the stirrup leathers very short and fasten them to the girth with string or spur straps so they do not flap about. The reins can be passed through the irons, which stops them slipping down the horse's sides and getting tangled round his legs.

Get the horse used to the long reins in his stable first. Fasten one to the nearside ring on the cavesson – not the bit – with the loops gathered in your hand, and get a helper to hold him and if necessary reassure him while you let it touch his back and quarters. His stance will show you how he feels about this: head up and ears flicking back to you means he is not sure what is happening, but as he relaxes his head will go down and his ears will flick forwards. Now pass the rein round his quarters so it touches the top of his hindleg, moving it gently up and down until he accepts that there is nothing to worry about. Get your assistant to move him round the box a few steps and then stop when you give him the voice commands.

Now do the same from the other side and finally with both reins on, attached to the left and right cavesson rings. You should stand behind him but slightly to the side; once

Introducing the horse to long reins, being careful not to startle him by flapping them suddenly round his quarets and hindlegs.

he accepts this (and there is no reason why he should find it any big deal) you can move out to your enclosed area. Get your assistant to stay at his head until he gets the hang of the idea, though all the voice commands should be given by you.

Some people like to carry a whip when long reining, but unless you are very experienced there are two disadvantages to this. One is that your hands will already be full with the long reins and it is something else to cope with; the other is that if you tap the horse to encourage him forwards you have to stand so close that you could get kicked if he objects.

The 'classic' way of introducing long reining is to start on a circle, so that you are lungeing with an inside and an outside rein. However, it is often easier to start by going straight and, if you wish, to move on to a circle when the horse understands what is being asked of him and is happy with the contact of the two reins along his body. If you go large round the school he will follow the line of the fence and you can practice walk – halt – walk transitions.

If the horse is wearing a saddle and you long rein on a circle (which is really lungeing with two reins so that you have an inside and an outside rein) do not put the long rein through the stirrups. If you do, you will find that you are pulling backwards on the inside rein every time you give a signal. Instead, remove the stirrups and put on an overgirth to stop the saddle flaps flapping about.

When long reining on the straight, stand just far enough away so that there is no danger of you being kicked, and slightly to one side. On the left rein, you should be slightly to the left and on the right, slightly to the right. This means that he can see you (which he cannot if you stand directly behind him) and gives you more control if anything goes wrong. If he decides to take off and you are standing behind, you have no control at all – but if you are slightly to one side, you have a much better chance of influencing him. If the worst comes to the worst, you can drop the outside rein and pull on the inside one with both hands.

Working from the side may seem theoretically wrong when one of the basic aims of ridden work is for the horse to go straight. But as long as you change your position occasionally on the straight and make sure that you stand to the right for right turns and to the left for left ones, you will not risk the horse becoming any more one-sided than he is naturally. (Horses are inevitably stiffer on one side than the other; most find it easier to work on the left rein than the right. One school of thought says that this is because we tend to handle them more from the left, which is farther proof that horses should be handled from both sides. Another believes that it is all to do with the way the foetus curls inside its dam.)

Try and keep a light but steady contact on the long reins, with your elbows bent. When you ask for a turn, you have to ask earlier than if you were at the horse's head; flex with the inside rein and allow with the outside one. As you change direction and change your position, the new outside rein will come into contact with his quarters: he may jump forwards in surprise, but try and go with him rather than pulling back and reassure him with your voice.

Two or three short sessions should see him getting the hang of things. Once he – and you – feel confident, you can attach the long reins to the bit. Keep the rein contact light and when you ask for halts or changes of direction, be careful about giving and taking rather than pulling. A competent long reiner can teach a horse to accept the bit and flex to the rein (a process often called 'putting a mouth on a horse') before a rider ever puts a foot in the stirrup.

Introduction to traffic

You need to be sure (or as sure as you ever can be with horses) that your youngster will not take fright at traffic before you long rein him round roads and tracks. Finding quiet routes becomes harder all the time, but fast, busy roads and horses do not make a good combination at the best of times. Some horses accept everything without turning a hair; others are wary of large or noisy vehicles to start with and need careful acclimatisation.

Some people believe in starting Traffic Training with capital Ts at the yearling stage. The problem with this approach is that a yearling often does not have the maturity to cope with such a potentially stressful experience. Stick to traffic training with small ts until he is older – if possible, turn him out in a field by a road with a sensible companion so that he can see and hear vehicles going past. Walk him past parked cars on the way from the field to the stableyard, first with the engine turned off and later with it running. Once he accepts this, walk him past a car with the door open; get someone to open and close the door and get in and out while he watches, and so on.

You have a head start if you keep your horse on a farm or a yard where tractors or agricultural machinery are used. Horses get so used to seeing all the comings and goings that venturing out into the real world is not such a shock. A quiet environment is very nice, but you can have too much of a good thing.

Once you have bitted your two-year-old and he is good to lead, take him out with an older, totally reliable horse so that he can see traffic and other distractions. Play safe: try and pick a spot where he can graze whilst cars and other vehicles go past, but there is no danger of him taking fright and leaping out into the road. When you feel confident that he is confident, lead him round quiet routes with his schoolmaster.

Never lead a horse on the roads in a headcollar, as you do not have enough control. Make sure you can be seen by wearing a fluorescent tabard with a suitable message, such as 'Slow Please, Young Horse'. A friend of one of the authors found that she got the best results of all by wearing a plain fluorescent tabard with L-plates fastened front and back – non-horsey motorists do not always realise why they should slow down for a young horse, but everyone knows that L-plates signify inexperience. She did get a bit fed up with people who asked when she was going to take her test, but reckoned that this was a small price to pay!

Always lead or ride a horse on the left hand side of the road, so you are facing oncoming vehicles, and put yourself between him and the traffic. This means that you have a better chance of stopping his quarters from swinging out into the road, especially if you carry a schooling whip in your right hand. It presupposes, of course, that he must be used to being led from the offside – which you will have done right from the start.

Long reining outside

Once you feel that you are ready to venture outside, enlist the help of your school-master again; he can either be long reined or ridden. You may also want to have an assistant to walk at your horse's head the first few times, depending on the youngster's temperament and your experience and confidence. Pick short, quiet routes that take you round in a circle – it is always a mistake to take a young horse out and then turn round and come back the same way. This is virtually teaching him to nap: the time may come when he decides he has gone far enough, thank you, and would rather turn round and go home.

When the horse is more experienced, he can be long reined round the fields and later round the fields and later round the roads. Here the hedge is a useful barrier

Start off with the young horse behind his companion, then as he gains confidence allow him to come alongside and eventually take the lead for short periods. He must learn right from the start to accept whatever position you ask him to take. It is vital that the person riding or long reining the schoolmaster is on the ball and ready to move up and give a lead past anything that bothers the youngster. You do not want a confrontation, and if your companion can anticipate possible problems you can get past them before the young horse has chance to think about stopping or trying to whip round.

You have to accept that your horse will want to gawk at everything, but use your voice to keep him going forwards. He may be so busy looking at everything around him that he spends a lot of time tripping over his own feet. Some people like to put on knee boots as well as brushing ones, in case the horse slips and comes down on the road, but they have to be fastened very carefully to ensure that they will neither slip down nor rub. The last thing you want is a young horse dancing a tarantella down the road because one of his knee boots is dangling round a fetlock.

When you are as sure as you can be that your horse is confident and happy, take him out on his own – perhaps bringing your assistant back to walk at his head for the first few outings. Pick a short, quiet, familiar route that should be free from hazards: though Sod's Law dictates that the first time you go out on your own is the first time you meet a steam roller, or discover that a herd of cows has been turned out in a previously empty field.

Chapter 6
Backing

The first time a rider actually gets on your young horse will seem like a momentous occasion. For both your sakes, try and think of it as just the latest step in his education. It is essential that whoever gets on him is reasonably agile and totally confident, so if you are likely to be nervous about it, be honest and find someone who is not. A reasonably lightweight jockey is obviously better than someone who is an ideal candidate for Weight Watchers, but there is no need to be paranoid about it: a three-year-old riding horse is very different from a Thoroughbred yearling destined for the racetrack.

There are different schools of thought on when to back a horse. Some trainers like to leave it until the horse is three, whereas others prefer to back their two-year-olds. Really it depends on your horse's development: if he is big and strong, it may be perfectly all right to back him at two as long as you do not start riding him properly. No matter how big and strong he looks to be, his bones are still growing and you could cause permanent damage by riding him too early. Flat racehorses are, of course, backed as yearlings and raced as two-year-olds – but this is purely a matter of economics and no one would pretend that it is the best thing for the horse. You must also remember that racehorses are fed very differently from ordinary riding horses, and are only ridden by lightweights.

Prepare your horse for backing right from the start by putting an arm over his back while you are grooming him and leaning against him. Stand at his side on a low box and do the same thing, then progress to a proper mounting block. This gets him used to you being higher up than he is; if a horse is frightened when he is backed for the first time, it is usually not because of the unaccustomed weight but because he is startled by the sight of someone above him. The theory is that predators in the wild will leap onto a horse's back, so his reaction is an instinctive one. You can also get him used to you standing at his side and making small jumps off the gound; you may feel like an idiot but once he accepts you bouncing up and down he is also likely to accept you having a leg-up.

Some people like to back a horse in the stable, but unless it has a very high roof the danger here is that if he does panic and go up, the would-be rider and handler are both in vulnerable positions. You are usually safer using the enclosed area in which he is used to being worked; work him on the lunge or long reins first,so that he settles, then get ready to back him in.

There is no reason why you cannot back a horse bareback; some trainers like to do this with pyhysically mature two-year-olds who have not yet been introduced to wearing a saddle. If wearing a saddle is second nature, then before you attempt to get on him, check that the girth is tight enough (if it has loosened while the horse has been lunged, you will feel very silly if the saddle slips as soon as you settle in place).

(Pages 69 to 71) Backing a three-year-old. His ears flicked back, showing that he is paying attention to what is happening, and his head comes up as he feels the rider's weight – but he soon settles.

Ideally three people should be involved in the backing process – one to hold the horse and reassure him, one to get on him and one to leg-up and support the rider. Everyone must be experienced enough to monitor the horse's reactions and know when he is wary but happy to accept what is happening and when he needs to be given time to settle.

The holder stands at the horse's head on the nearside, so that if he moves away or jumps forward there is no danger of getting jumped on. She holds the cheekpiece – not the reins – whilst the rider stands at the horse's side, talks to him and pats him on both

sides, leaning an arm over the saddle and putting weight on it – all of which the horse should be used to. The rider then positions herself to take a leg-up, leaving the reins on the horse's neck: during the backing process the holder controls the horse and the rider is simply a weight he has to adjust to.

The legger-up needs to be strong enough to take most of the rider's weight for a short period, as at first he supports more of it than the horse. A quiet, careful leg-up puts the rider halfway over the front of the saddle; the horse is less likely to object to the weight being over the front of the saddle than if it is placed farther back. It is important that the legger-up takes most of the rider's weight to start with, so the horse can get used to the idea. If the horse stays calm, the rider stays in that position for a few seconds then is lowered to the ground; if he seems worried, she should be let down without any fuss and the process repeated as the horse relaxes.

With wary or nervous horses, that is sometimes enough for the first time. Bring him out again later that day or the next day and do the same again, and keep on doing it until he accepts that there is nothing to fear. If he is the sort who accepts it all with equanimity – and most do – you can carry on to the next stage.

Whenever you are teaching a horse something, you should start by repeating the previous lesson. Backing is no exception, so start by letting the legger-up support most of the weight and gradually let the horse take over. Eventually he will be supporting the rider as she lays across the saddle with the legger-up ready to help her slip down if he becomes uneasy. He can then be walked round with the rider leaning over the saddle and the helper at her side.

The horse may step forwards or sideways because he is puzzled at the sudden weight;

if he stays calm, the rider can stay in place as the horse is walked forwards. She should only slip off if the horse is worried: you do not want him to think that he only has to take a step forwards to get rid of the weight. If this all seems rather boring, so much the better – you want the horse to think that it is no big deal.

When he accepts all that has gone before, put on a neckstrap. The rider can be legged up on to a saddle with the stirrup irons run down the leathers and gently put her left foot in the iron. She can gradually put more weight on it, and when the horse is calm and accepting of the process she can carefully swing her right leg over to sit in the saddle. She must be very careful not to touch the horse with her right toe as her leg swings over, and land as lightly as possible.

It is vital for the rider to stay leaning forwards, so the horse is not frightened by something suddenly appearing above him. She should keep her legs resting lightly by his side, stroke his shoulders and talk to him while the holder also makes a fuss of him. The advantage of this method is that the rider can judge the horse's reactions to her putting weight on the stirrup, and thus judge the right moment to progress to swinging her leg over his back.

In theory the horse should stay calm enough for the holder to lead him round in a small circle, with the rider still leaning forwards and the legger-up at her side. The rider should not attempt to give any leg aids, just keep her legs lightly against his sides so he gets used to the feel of them as he moves. The holder brings him to a halt and gives him a titbit whilst the rider slips carefully out of the saddle.

When the horse stays relaxed and accepts his rider's weight, she can gradually assume a more upright position. The key word is 'gradually' – remember that any sudden movements above him will startle the horse, so do not sit up suddenly or wave your arms about.

The good news is that nine times out of ten, everything goes smoothly and easily and you are all left wondering what all the fuss was about. The bad news is that occasionally you get a horse who says that he does not really like this idea and decides that the quickest way round it is to get rid of his rider. All the latter can do is try and hang on – which is where a neckstrap is very useful – whilst the holder does the same at the front end, talking to the horse at the same time in an effort to calm him down. Obviously it is best not to let the horse realise that he can get rid of his unwelcome burden, but if you cannot help parting company, settle him down again and go back to the beginning of the backing process.

Most horses draw the line at a buck and/or a plunge; the real monsters are few and far between. If you do draw the short straw and find yourself with one of the latter, get expert help rather than keep trying and failing. It may hurt your pride (and other bits) but the more often the horse gets away with it, the harder it is to cure.

If you do decide you need help, pick your expert carefully. Just because someone has a string of fancy qualifications it does not mean that he or she is an expert on young horses. You are far better going to someone with a good reputation locally, perhaps a reputable dealer or 'nagsman' – the sort of person who is backing and bringing on young horses all the time and knows how to cope with problems safely.

It is essential to be honest; it is not fair to pretend that no one has ever tried to get on the horse if he has spent several days perfecting his technique in getting rid of prospective jockeys. Forewarned is forearmed – and in any case, anyone who is used to young horses will soon be able to tell if he or she is being asked to pick up the pieces.

So much for the negative side of the coin . . . remember that if you take things sensibly, the chances are that your horse will do the same.

First sessions

Now your horse is well on the way to being ridden, and you will be surprised how quickly you make progress in the early stages. For the first few sessions, it makes sense to lunge him for ten minutes before you get on him – it gives him chance to let off steam with a buck and a kick if he feels like it, and gets his brain in gear and into 'work mode' by asking him to respond to your voice commands.

(Pages 73 and 74) The rider sits quietly, with his weight slightly forwards and off the horse's back, as a helper leads him forwards.

At first you will need to ride in your enclosed area, as the boundaries compensate for the rudimentary steering. Be prepared for the fact that your horse will feel wobbly and uncoordinated; remember that your weight on his back alters his centre of gravity and he has to learn to compensate for that. It also means that you have to have a reasonably secure seat, because if you lose your balance it makes it much harder for the horse to adjust his.

If you have long reined him from the bit, he should be confident enough in your hands to ride as normal. If for any reason you did not want to do this or are worried about riding straight off the bit, use 'back-up' reins fixed to the side rings of a lungeing cavesson. Fit the bridle as for lungeing, and use one pair of reins going to the cavesson rings and another to the bit rings. Hold them as you would the reins of a double bridle, with the cavesson reins as your top pair and the bit ones as the bottom reins. You can then use nose pressure (something the horse will already be used to) as well as bit pressure, thus lessening the risk of inadvertently socking him in the teeth.

Riding a young horse is a bit like teaching someone a new language. Your instructions must be clear, and you must give him the chance to obey them. If he does not understand, you repeat the same aids until the idea clicks. Use what he already understands – your voice aids – in association with leg aids, rein aids and shifts in your bodyweight; eventually you will be able to dispense with the voice aids except when you need something 'extra.'

However, this does not mean that voice aids are not important. They can be a vital means of communication, especially when a horse is worried or excited; talking to him in a soothing voice can have more effect than anything else. It seems peculiarly illogical that riders in dressage competitions are penalised for using their voices but allowed to carry whips and wear spurs, even at the most basic level.

Your aids should be definite but not harsh. Keep them as light as possible, right from the start; if you squeeze the horse like a vice the first time you ask him to walk on he will either shoot off in surprise or stand still in amazement. If he does the latter, you have nothing in reserve when you repeat the aid. If a light aid produces no response, then use a slightly stronger one – and as soon as he obeys, stop asking.

Some horses are easier to start with if you let your helper walk round with you, though he or she should not lead the horse or give any voice commands. Others pick up the idea right from the start, though you should for safety's sake have someone else with you. At first the horse will naturally hang to the fence round the schooling area; make your first turns wide and ask for them in plenty of time, opening your hand to the inside without pulling back.

Unless you are incredibly lucky and have a fantastically well balanced horse, your youngster will feel as if he is going downhill. This is because he is carrying his and your weight on his forehand, so do not make things worse by leaning forwards. Try and sit straight with a light contact on the reins – remembering that this does not mean keeping your hands perfectly still. Your horse's head moves: your hands and arms have to move with it, or you will be checking him in the mouth at every stride.

Turns should be wide and gradual; look where you want to go so that your bodyweight influences the horse and open your hand in the direction of your turn. It is important that when you open your hand, you do not pull back at the same time – if you do, you are effectively asking and blocking at the same time.

Ask him to halt by giving the familiar voice command, sitting tall and closing your fingers round the reins. As he slows, relax your fingers and allow him to go forwards to halt. You might have to ask two or three times at first until he understands, but you should always aim to resist the forward motion rather than pull back.

When you trot for the first time, ask when the horse is going towards the gate. Do not hustle him into it: it is far better if he falls into trot at the first few attempts rather than leaps forward and throws you off balance. You want to avoid coming down suddenly on his back, which may startle him into shooting forwards and set off a chain reaction of imbalance.

Use an open rein to help steer a young horse. Rotate the elbow so that the rein goes to the side, but there is no backwards pull.

Your body should be slightly in front of the vertical as you rise, and you should let his movement push you out of the saddle rather than stand up and down in the stirrups. (If this is starting to sound like a textbook in basic riding, it is because most of us fall into bad habits which riding young horses highlights quite dramatically!) He will probably trot for a few strides than fall back to walk, which is exactly what you want him to do.

Some horses find it very difficult to find their balance in trot, and go faster as they fall more on to their forehand. It is not that they are running away, more that they cannot help themselves – a bit like a ball gaining momentum as it rolls downhill. The rider can help by slowing the rhythm of her rising so it is behind the horse's stride: he will slow down to try and match his rhythm to hers. All trot work must be done rising; a horse can only take a rider in sitting trot when he is stronger and better balanced, and even then it should only be for a few strides at a time.

After two or three sessions, the horse should start to get the basic idea. Some find cantering more exciting than trotting: if a horse is going to throw a buck, then the strike-off to canter is the most likely time. For this reason, you may prefer to introduce cantering on the lunge before you ask for the new pace under saddle. Do not worry if he runs into it at first, but make sure you give him plenty of room by walking a small circle whilst he describes a large one. The last thing you want is a horse struggling to keep his balance on a tight circle and putting strain on his hocks at the same time.

You may find it easier to make your circle into a square when you ask for canter. By lungeing at one end of your working area you can ask him to trot down the long side, and go into the corner. If your trot is active enough and your voice command brisk enough, you should be able to get him to canter going into the corner, and nine times out of ten he will strike off on the correct leg and you can then move back on to a big

The rider has just asked this horse to canter going into a corner.

circle. If he goes on the wrong leg, do not worry too much. Finesse comes later, and you should not bring him back to trot immediately in the way you would with an advanced horse. Let him canter for a few strides – ignoring any bucks – and when he settles, you will probably find that he falls back into trot quite quickly of his own accord.

As soon as he understands the voice aids for canter and strikes off without exploding, you can ask for canter under saddle. Always ask going into a corner to start with, and use your voice in conjunction with the normal aids. Keep your weight out of the saddle so you are cantering in half seat, so that again you are not asking him to take more than he can physically cope with. When you come back to trot, start rising straight away; if you try and sit, his head will go up, his back will hollow and he will be tense and off balance.

Keep your weight off the horse's back when you first start cantering to make it easier for him.

Once you start riding your horse, it is tempting to try and make progress with basic schooling. However, nothing is guaranteed to make a horse bored more quickly than riding round a school *ad infinitum*, and if he gets bored he is either going to switch off and stop listening to you or look for trouble. As soon as your young horse is rideable – which means simply that you can stop, start and turn – you should get him riding out with another horse.

This will mean getting him shod for the first time to lessen the risk of bruised soles; to start with, have shoes put on the front feet but not the back ones. It makes for an easier introduction to shoeing for the horse, and minimises the damage to other horses if he becomes involved in a kicking match out in the field. He will not be doing enough road work in these very early stages to cause any damage to his feet, but if you are worried about your particular horse, take your farrier's advice.

If you have previously long reined the horse round quiet roads, riding out will be just a variation on a familiar theme; even so, it must be approached with forethought and common sense. You need to call on the services of your schoolmaster horse and his rider again, and to find a route that is quiet and reasonably short. Aim to go out for about half an hour to 40 minutes, so the horse has a proper outing but is not on his knees with exhaustion by the time you get back.

Ride him in the school for ten minutes to begin with, so he is listening to you and you can reinforce the idea of what going forwards, stopping and turning mean. Then you can set off into the wide world for the first time, with the schoolmaster in front going out of the yard and the young horse fairly close behind. Pick a route that is short, quiet and which takes you in a circle: do not ride down the road, turn round and come back the same way, because this is inviting the youngster to nap. If he thinks it is acceptable to turn round, the time will come when he decides to do it of his own accord because he does not want to go any further!

When you have plenty of visibility in front and behind on the roads it is often safer to ride alongside each other, with the young horse on the inside, as drivers who might be prepared to pass horses in single file at speed will be forced to slow down for two abreast. Come back to single file well before any bends. Fluorescent tabards make you more visible; the other useful piece of safety equipment is a spare stirrup leather buckled round as a neckstrap.

If the young horse is hesitant or worried about traffic going past, position him so that he is on the inside of his companion, with his nose about level with the rider's knee. This way, the schoolmaster acts as both a shield and a lead. If the youngster is bold and curious – as many are – he may want to step out in front. Let him, but make sure that your escort is ready to come straight past and give him a lead at the slightest sign of hesitation. You do not want a confrontation at this stage, you want everything to be nice and easy.

You may find that you do not go out of walk on the first ride, but that does not matter. Your aim is to keep the horse going forwards, but not to hustle him. If he feels confident and your ride takes you along a suitable track, then try a short trot. The going must be good and the terrain either level or slightly uphill: your young horse will have so much to take in anyway that you do not want him to tackle the complexities of trotting down slopes on his first ride out.

If you look back over the past few weeks you will probably be amazed at how much progress you have made in a short time. Spend the next few weeks simply consolidating what your horse has learned. Your aims should be very basic at this stage – you want him to learn to go forwards from the leg, calmly and with a good rhythm. Forget about the niceties of head carriage and outline; all that comes later. At present it is quite enough for your three-year-old to carry you confidently.

Some horses are naturally well balanced and find it all quite easy. Others feel as if they have five legs and are closely related to the crab; they wobble about all over the place, fall over their own feet and are generally uncoordinated. Big horses, who take longer to mature physically, are usually 'worse' in this respect than smaller, naturally more agile ones. All you can do is give them time.

When your youngster has done about four to six weeks' easy work, you have to decide whether to turn him away and give him a complete break or keep him ticking over. Giving him a rest often makes a lot of sense; he has learned a lot in a short time and has had demands put on him mentally as well as physically. Backing a horse in spring or early summer, working him gently until the end of the summer and then turning him away until the spring of his fourth year has a lot to recommend it.

Part Two
Schooling

Chapter 7
Early Schooling

By the time your horse reaches the Spring of his fourth year he will be ready for more serious work. If he has been turned away for the winter, start with a refresher course to remind him of everything he learned the previous year. In some ways he will find things easier, as he will have matured physically (and hopefully, mentally!) But you will still have to give him chance to adapt to your weight again and to find out how to balance himself.

It is important that whoever rides a young horse is a help, not a hindrance, to him finding his balance. It is all too easy to get a vicious circle: the horse loses his balance momentarily, which throws the rider off balance and causes the horse even more problems. Riding a youngster is not a matter of demonstrating the perfect textbook position – though the classical principles are still the best ones – but of giving him clear signals and positioning your weight in a way that helps him obey.

It often helps the rider's balance to adjust the stirrups a hole shorter than the length that would be adopted on a well-schooled horse. Your legs must be round and in contact with the horse's sides all the time; it is a mistake to take your legs away from a 'forward going' horse in the belief that this will slow him down. A lot of youngsters rush because they are on their forehand and losing their balance, not because they are running away from the rider's legs.

Many young horses are not at all forward going when they are first ridden, simply because they are not sure where to go. Once you have got past the initial 'wobbly' stage, start to ask for a quicker reaction to your aids. The easiest way is to use a schooling whip – though not one of the extra long variety that reaches all the way to the horse's hocks! Make sure that you can use it only when you want to; if you ride round inadvertently tapping the horse you will probably get a reaction, but not the one you wanted.

Get the horse used to you carrying a short stick before trotting off regardless with your schooling whip; get an assistant to stand at his head while you hold it out to the side and carefully change it from one hand to the other. The accepted method of changing over a whip, i.e. reversing it over the withers, should only be used when the horse is happy for you to carry it, move it about slightly and in contact should be light but steady.

A short stick is the only sort that should be carried for jumping. Some riders prefer it for hacking out whilst others opt for a schooling whip: the advantage of a schooling whip is that it is used without taking a hand of the reins, whereas with a short stick you must take your hand off the rein to avoid jabbing the horse in the mouth as you use it.

Once the horse is happy for you to carry a schooling whip and move it around, use it to teach him to be smarter off the leg aids. Close your legs round his sides, and if he does not answer immediately, give a definite tap on the girth with the schooling whip. You are not hitting him, but nor should the action be so hesitant he does not feel it. Be sure that you allow with your hands at the same time;he may be so surprised that he shoots forwards, and you do not want to say 'Go' with one set of aids and 'Stop' with another.

As long as he goes forwards smartly, praise him and give him a pat. If he takes no notice, do the same again – but this time make the tap much sharper. Eventually he will get the message, and will soon pay the same attention to your leg aids alone. Keep him up to the mark; if he lapses back into his old ways, remind him how he should respond. This technique works equally well with older horses: it is amazing how many people let their horses think about it before moving off from the leg.

The rein contact with a young horse should be light but consistent. A lot of riders trot round with their reins hanging in loops in the belief that this is keeping a light hand, but you need to have a light contact between the horse's mouth and your hands so that the signals you give are clear cut. An 'on-off' contact means that the aids are a surprise to the horse rather than a system of signals he has confidence in.

People often ask how 'strong' the contact should be. 'Strong' is really the wrong word to use – the last thing you want is a pulling contest, or to feel that you are holding the horse's head up for him. Aim for a light but steady feel, rather than a dead weight: this means keeping your shoulders, arms, elbows and hands supple. Keep your fingers closed round the reins, without gripping, with thumbs on top and palms tilted slightly upwards so you can see your fingernails – this will help you achieve the desired suppleness.

An awful lot is talked and written about the necessity of keeping a 'still hand'. If you follow this advice to the letter you are actually catching your horse in the mouth with every stride he takes. What is really needed is a following hand; watch a horse moving and you will see that his head moves with every stride, especially in walk and canter. By following that motion (which will require slight, but not exaggerated movements) you will keep the desirable 'elastic' contact.

The old maxim of having a straight line from the bit, through your hands to your elbows actually makes a lot of sense. This position gives you the greatest flexibility and suppleness; straight arms are stiff arms and stiff arms lead to an uncomfortable and therefore resisting horse. However, you also have to take into account your horse's natural head carriage. If he carries his head high, your hands will need to be relatively high; if he carries it low, your hands will need to be lower than in the previous case.

At this stage, forget about trying to establish a 'proper' head carriage. Your only priority should be free, forwards movement: if you start trying to establish an outline before this is achieved the horse will back off. Right from the beginning, you should think about riding from the leg into the hand.

Although it may sound obvious, make sure you keep your hands on the appropriate sides of the horse's neck. One of the commonest riding faults – at all standards – is to cross the inside hand over the withers in an attempt to get the horse to turn. This blocks the forward movement and leads to confusion all round. There have even been occasions – and no doubt will be more in the future – when a desperate rider has had to drop one rein, put both hands on the other and abandon any pretence at finesse in order to steer a horse safely! Desperate situations call for desperate remedies, but luckily they do not arise too often.

If your steering is wonky, do not forget how helpful an aid the open rein can be. Moving your hand out to the side in the direction in which you want to turn is a simple but effective technique, as long as you remember not to pull back at the same time. Remember, too, that the outside hand must allow the horse to turn: if you ask with the inside rein without giving on the outside one, you will be saying 'Yes' with one hand and 'No' with the other.

Your bodyweight is one of the most vital aids. By simply looking in the direction in which you want to go, you will shift your weight slightly. As the horse's natural reaction is to shift his weight to match yours, you have given an aid almost without realising it. Working to the same principle, it follows that you can inadvertently confuse the horse by shifting your weight without meaning to. If you sit lopsided, you cannot help but make your horse lopsided as well. Riding a young horse is a surefire way of showing up the bad habits we all lapse into, so it is a good idea to get someone who knows what they are looking for to watch you.

Ninety-nine point nine per cent of your trot work should be done rising, as the horse is not yet ready to take your weight sitting for long periods. As he becomes more established, you can introduce sitting trot, but only for a couple of strides at a time. Keep your weight light and do not try to sit deep into the saddle, or he will hollow against you.

The more used your horse becomes to making transitions, the better balanced he will become. Eventually you will be able to make barely perceptible half halts as part of the progress towards riding him on the bit, but at first transitions will be gradual. He needs time not only to take in your instructions but to carry them out. It is a bit like learning a foreign language; at first it takes a while to mentally translate, but as you become more fluent the translation becomes instantaneous.

It is important to keep thinking forwards even when you are changing to a slower pace, so that you maintain the impulsion. It is also important that you are quite clear in your mind about the difference between impulsion (controlled energy) and speed. Downward transitions are always harder than upward ones, but if you concentrate on riding forwards into a restraining hand – and allowing the hand as soon as the horse obeys – rather than pulling back, you will be on the right lines.

No matter how big and well developed your horse, he needs time to build up his muscles. Keep schooling sessions fairly short; 20 minutes to half an hour is long enough to get him working but not so long that he grows tired and/or bored. Two or three short sessions a week in the school are quite enough; you need to build up the horse's range of experience and keep his interest by hacking him out regularly.

A lot of trainers spend most of their time working in trot, but the four-year-old has got to learn to canter with a rider on his back . . . and the only way he learns is through practice. Some horses have a naturally balanced canter, whereas others make you wonder if they are related to the giraffe family. If yours belongs in the first category, count your blessings; if he falls in the second, console yourself with the fact that it is just a matter of time.

Establish a reasonably energetic trot before you think of asking for canter. Young horses need more 'oomph' to achieve canter than mature, well-schooled ones who can put their hindlegs further underneath them. Give your horse room: circles should be at least 20 metres in diameter and the horse should also be cantered right round the perimeter of the school so he gets used to maintaining the pace.

You should now be working on getting accurate strike-offs on the correct leg, without making a fuss or hustling the horse. Ask as you are going into the corner of the school, being clear with your aids. In theory the outside leg is the one that asks for canter and the inside one is used to ask the horse to go forwards, but in practice a lot of horses do not like the feel of the outside leg at first and swing or even jump away from it. The result is that they bend to the outside rather than the inside and strike off on the wrong leg.

If your horse fits this description, forget about using the outside leg at first – he can learn to accept it later, when he is cantering happily. Instead, think about dropping your weight to your inside knee, which will mean that you move your inside seatbone slightly forwards without stiffening through your body.

The inside hands asks for a slight bend and the outside hand allows it; problems often arise because a rider is trying to 'support with the outside rein' and ends up restricting with it, so the horse is in effect being asked to bend and prevented from doing so at the same time.

Mounting from the ground

So far you have always been given a leg-up on to your horse. Now you can teach him to accept being mounted in the 'normal' way – and once taught, do it as little as possible! No matter how lightweight and agile you are, every time you mount from the ground you are pulling the saddle over, putting stress on the horse's back and possibly even twisting the saddle tree.

It is much better to use a mounting block or get a leg-up as a matter of routine. However, as there will be times when you have no choice but to get on from the ground, you have to accustom the horse to this. Start with a mounting block, which he will already be used to, and get an assistant to hold the cheekpiece of the horse's bridle (not the reins – if he pulls back and catches himself in the mouth it may cause more trouble than it prevents.)

Get on with as much agility as you can muster, being careful not to dig him in the stomach with your toe or brush his quarters with your right foot as you swing it over, and sink lightly into the saddle. He must stand still while you get on and pick up the reins, but do not keep him hanging about too long to start with. Standing still is something a lot of young horses do not take kindly to at first, and you do not want to set up a battle.

It is far better to stand for a couple of seconds and then move off than to try and insist that he stands for a long time; if he starts fidgeting, trying to walk off or walk backwards you can end up with him getting so fed up that he threatens to – or even worse, actually does – rear. You can ask him to stand still for a little longer every time you get on, so that he gets used to waiting while you adjust the girth and so on.

Tack

You may find that you want to re-think the tack you are using according to your horse's early reactions and perhaps change the bit and/or noseband. Some horses accept a bit right from the start whilst others are fussy or 'gobby' all the way through the teething process. Different horses have different ways of showing resistance or resentment; some swish their tails, some grind their teeth and some open their mouths to try and get away from any sort of contact. To a certain extent, you have to ignore it in the knowledge that as the horse matures and finds what you are asking him to do easier, he will usually become more settled in his mouth.

You do not want to be chopping and changing bits too much at this early stage, but if you are having real problems it is better to try something different to see if the horse is happier. There is no hard and fast rule that says that every horse must go in a certain type of snaffle – and whilst thick mouthpieces are theoretically milder, some horses prefer less bulk in their mouths and go much more nicely in a thinner one. It is also worth reminding yourself that any bit is only as mild, or as strong, as the hands on the reins!

At the moment he is experimenting as to what is most comfortable (or to be more accurate, what is the best way of coping with the piece of metal or plastic that has been put in his mouth.) Do not be paranoid about keeping his mouth shut: remember that he needs to be able to move his jaw and that if you strap his mouth shut too tight you may simply give him something else to set himself against. On the other hand, if he tries to go round like a fish out of water you have to show him that this is not acceptable.

A dry mouth is an unresponsive mouth; if he is forever opening his in an attempt to evade the bit there will be no saliva to lubricate the movement of the bit over the bars and the result will be a bruised, sore mouth and an even more unhappy horse. If this sounds like your horse, give him a mint before you get on him – or tie a Polo to the centre of your bit with a piece of cotton! You may find that a correctly fitted Flash or drop noseband helps. Fasten it loosely to start with then adjust it, if necessary.

A selection of snaffles which may be suitable for a young horse. From left, a D-ring snaffle with copper and steel rollers, a loose ring snaffle, a rubber-covered loose ring snaffle, a rubber-covered loose ring snaffle, a full cheek snaffle with French link mouthpiece and a Nathe snaffle with a flexible plastic mouthpiece. The stainless steel, loose ring snaffle is often a good one to start with.

Double check that your bit fits correctly and that the mouthpiece is neither too fat nor too thin for the conformation of his mouth. A horse with a short mouth or a fat tongue cannot take a thick mouthpiece and is often happier with a thinner one (perhaps the bridoon of a double bridle) or a French link snaffle. Some horses do not like jointed mouthpieces at all but take quite happily to mullen ones; if yours comes into this category he may like a Nathe snaffle. This is made from a strong but flexible plastic that is said to encourage the horse to take a contact and to salivate.

A bit with D-cheeks or full cheeks helps with steering, but again you have to weigh this against the horse's conformation. If your horse has a workmanlike to heavy head, you may find that the standard designs of full cheek snaffles pinch and press at the top, causing a lot of discomfort. The best designs are angled away from the horse's face at the top, but even this may not be enough.

Some horses spend a lot of time drawing back their tongues, which again can result in a dry mouth. A lot of young horses like jointed snaffles with alternate copper and steel rollers; they like the taste of the copper and the rollers give them something to play with, so they stop drawing back their tongues or at least do it to a lesser extent. Alternatively, the joint of a cheek snaffle with keepers sits higher on the tongue than that of an ordinary snaffle, which may solve the problem – taking into consideration the possible problem with this kind of cheekpiece mentioned before.

Get an expert to check that your saddle sits behind his shoulders and does not interfere with his movement, and that there is sufficient clearance of the withers with a rider on board: a good saddler who understands horse anatomy and movement is the best source of advice, but is not always easy to find. The gullet must be wide enough to avoid pressure on the dorsal spinous processes and the panels shaped to spread your weight over a wide area, not concentrate it on on a small one and thus cause pressure points. The flocking must be even and there must not be too much of it; too many saddles are overstuffed.

You will always get some movement, but it should not bounce up and down or slip from side to side. In theory a saddle should be level when looked at from the side, not tilting forwards or backwards, but in practice it may look as if it tilts forwards because your horse does exactly that. A growing youngster will go through stages when he is higher behind than in front – a good saddler will help you get the best possible fit for his stage of growth and muscle development and suggest when the saddle will need checking again.

Hacking out

Hacking out, both alone and in company, is a vital part of your young horse's education. It should be looked on as part of his normal work, albeit an enjoyable part – not as 'time of'. All too often you hear people say that they like their horses to be able to relax on a hack; in theory that is fine, because a relaxed horse can still be obedient and balanced. All too often, though, a 'relaxing' hack means the horse slopping along on a loose rein, falling over its own feet and paying attention to everything but the rider.

The golden rule is that whenever you ride your horse, he must pay attention to you. It is all very well doing beautiful work in a schooling area with no distractions – but the real world is not like that! Think ahead to the time when you want to compete, take part in sponsored rides, hunt, hack out with friends or whatever: if the horse's mind is boggled by all the distractions, you are going to have a very uncomfortable time. But if getting out and about, seeing the sights and learning to listen to his rider despite such distractions has been part and parcel of his education, you will have far fewer problems.

Most of your hacking will be at walk; trotting on the roads puts unnecessary concussion on limbs and feet, so save trotting for bridlepaths and tracks with good going. When you decide to try your first canter 'outdoors', pick your time and your place with care, as explained later in this section.

The horse's walk should bear the same hallmarks as all his other paces – free, forward movement with a good rhythm. He should be what racehorse trainers call 'on the bridle,' working from behind into a light contact.

It is often said that the walk is the hardest pace to improve and the easiest to spoil. The horse with a good stride at the walk must not be restricted because the rider is anxious to get him on the bit and starts fiddling with the reins to try and get the desired round outline. By the same token, the naturally short striding horse, such as a short-legged cob, should not be hustled out of his natural rhythm in an attempt to get him to walk out and lengthen his stride: all that will happen is that he will start to jog.

Your horse will learn to cope with different types of terrain through experience. Some could not care less about anything and wade through mud, puddles and everything else with great aplomb, whilst others are sure that horse-eating dragons lie under anything but tarmac. If your horse comes into the latter category, go round tiny puddles at first, for the simple reason that he will find it all too easy to jink round them. If you come to a wide puddle, get your escort horse to give you a lead through; keep your legs round the horse's sides and be prepared for the fact that he might decide to try and jump it. As long as you get to the other side, it does not matter, but you do not want to get left behind and sock him in the teeth.

Remember that everything is new to the young horse and be prepared for things that he may not like. That does not mean that you should both be looking for trouble, but it is as well to keep in mind that the things we take for granted when riding experienced horses can have quite a different effect on a youngster. For instance, some horses get worried the first time they are asked to go through stubble fields, presumably because of the prickling sensation. Others will jump the first few times that low twigs brush against the rider's coat.

A rider should always be looking ahead, and this is doubly important with a young horse. You need to 'read the road' as a good driver does so that you are aware of what lies ahead. As a precaution, fit a standing martingale and make sure that your cavesson noseband (or the cavesson part of your Flash) is a good, thick hunterweight one. Thin nosebands that do not stay in the correct place are useless and will not always stand up to the potential extra strain of having a martingale attached.

Take it steady and use your escort horse as a confidence builder. Whoever rides the escort must be just as alert as the young horse's rider: if the youngster is in front and shows signs of unease at something, the escort should come alongside and give him the confidence to go past.

Inevitably, the time will come when you will be out on your own and the horse says he does not like something – but by then he should have enough confidence in you to go forwards when asked. If you have to have a battle – and there are bound to be times when you will – then you must win, but there is no sense in looking for trouble when tact and quick thinking can defuse a potential problem.

Your youngster should learn to walk and trot in front, behind and beside his escort. If his trot becomes hurried, use your voice to steady him and slow the rhythm of your rising so you are slightly behind the movement; nine times out of ten, your horse will slow his pace to match your rhythm, because it is more comfortable for him to do so. If this does not work, use a series of checks and releases on the reins; avoid setting up a constant pull, because he will just use it to lean on your hands.

The first time you canter out in the open should ideally be when the horse has settled, not too early in the ride and not when he knows he is on the home stretch towards his field or a feed. Try and find a stretch that is slightly uphill, or at least on the level – cantering downhill, no matter how slight the gradient, puts the horse on his forehand.

The easiest way is to find somewhere that is wide enough for two horses to canter side by side. The escort horse must be steady enough not to buck or treat it as a potential race. Set up a nice active, balanced trot and ask for canter when you are ready; the young horse will usually take the other one's lead. If he is going to buck, it will be when he makes the transition from one pace to another, so get your weight slightly out of the saddle and stay there – if you try to sit to the canter right from the start the horse will probably hollow his back underneath you.

Ask for the canter lead that he finds easiest, but do not worry too much if you get the other one. Getting the correct strike-off on the straight will come easily enough later on: at the moment you should be happy with a reasonably controlled transition. It may all feel a bit wobbly and uncoordinated, but again, the refinements come later!

Allow plenty of room to come back to trot. Use your voice, as you did when the horse learned to canter on the lunge, coupled with light checks on the reins. He will probably fall into trot to a certain extent; it is only as he becomes more balanced and learns to put his hindlegs underneath himself that transitions will improve.

Most people have only a few places (if any) where it is safe to canter on a hack. Do not canter every time, or the horse will soon start to anticipate and will think 'This is where we canter' rather than wait for your aids.

Sooner or later, your young horse will have to learn to hack out on his own. Even if you intend to hack in company for 99 per cent of the time, he should ride out alone every now and again. There will inevitably be times when he has to be by himself, and it is far better to get him used to it from the start.

Wait until he has done a few rides with his escort and is going confidently in front round some short, quiet circuits. Pick a route that he is familiar with and keep it short, sweet and steady. He will probably be more hesitant than when he has company, but keep your legs round him and use your voice to encourage him. You may get funny looks from people who cannot understand why you are having a conversation with your horse, but ignore them.

Try and keep him going forwards – your first hack out alone is not a good time to stop and chat with a friend for ten minutes and possibly give your horse the idea that he does not really want to go any further. A brightly coloured tabard allows drivers to see you from as far away as possible, and hopefully to give you a wide berth. Try and ride confidently, but use your common sense – if you find a large vehicle coming towards you and there is a convenient field entrance, stand to one side whilst it goes past if you think your horse might be worried by it.

This is when your ability to 'read the road' will pay off. Look ahead for potential hazards such as spooky plastic bags in the hedge. Once you know they are there, look in the direction you intend to take as you approach them rather than directly at them. If you look at a plastic bag in the hedge or roadworks at the side of the road, the slight shift in your bodyweight will turn the horse towards it. If you ignore it and look at your route ahead, you will help your horse to do the same.

Chapter 8
Teaching the Young Horse to Jump

Jumping should be part of every horse's education, even if his eventual career is firmly earthbound. Apart from the fact that most horses enjoy jumping if they are introduced to it correctly, it has a beneficial effect on their flatwork. Jumping small fences calls for impulsion and concentration; it is amazing how the quality of the canter can be improved just by trotting over a small fence and letting the horse canter on landing. The push from the hocks needed to leave the ground helps achieve what we are looking for in the horse's flatwork: he will be working from behind, into the hand.

You can introduce a young horse to walking over poles on the ground at almost any stage of his education. On the Continent, it is common for trainers to loose school two-year-olds, yearlings and even foals over fences; this is done purely from a business point of view, to try and identify the youngsters with jumping potential as early as possible. The average owner, though, is better advised to wait until the horse is more mature.

All work puts strain on a horse's limbs, and the last thing you want is to put stress on undeveloped joints. Horses are good enough at damaging themselves on their own, without help from their trainers! If you want to try and find out whether a horse has a natural aptitude for jumping, then perhaps loose school him over a few small fences as a three-year-old; then leave it at that until he is four and better able to cope.

There are two schools of thought on whether or not loose schooling is an accurate guide to potential. It is always nice to see a horse that approaches a fence boldly and calmly and makes a classic bascule over it – but before you start booking your place in the Foxhunter final at Wembley, bear in mind that not all horses show the same jump under saddle as they do loose, even with a good rider. Nor should you automatically discount the big, gangly four-year-old who trips over his own feet, let alone a pole on the ground. There are plenty of horses who start off looking like disasters on four legs but turn out to have a decent jump when they are better balanced.

The first introduction to jumping is a simple pole on the ground. If the horse is a bold, sensible sort and the rider is competent and secure, he can be walked over it in the school as part of a normal work session. But if you want to introduce the idea of jumping before the horse is in ridden work, or prefer to play safe, start off on the lunge. The one proviso with this is that you must be competent and experienced at lungeing and you must be agile enough to move with the horse.

Professionals who are breaking and training horses all the time know when and how to take shortcuts. They also know that if the horse says no, they can cope with it – and that if he does a vertical take-off four feet into the air over the.pole on the ground, that they will not sock him in the teeth or land on his back like a ton of bricks (neither of which is recommended for either horse or rider's confidence and comfort.)

There is nothing to be ashamed of in playing safe, particularly if there are no pressures of time on you. Professional trainers may break a horse in March and be winning Newcomers competitions on it in May, but they have the time and the expertise. They also want results quickly, often so that the horse can get some winnings on its card straight away and be sold on.

Put a single pole down the long side of your school; if possible, have an assistant who can move it back into position if it gets kicked out. Start by lungeing your horse at the other end for 10 minutes so he settles down; he should be well away from the pole so that he does not learn to swerve round it. Then remove the side reins, if you have been using them, and fasten the lunge rein to the centre ring of the cavesson rather than the bit ring. The next bit is really exciting – you are going to lead him over the pole in walk.

There are times when gloves, a hard hat and boots with protective toe caps can lessen the risk of injury when dealing with young horses.

Boots with steel toe caps are an excellent investment for anyone dealing with horses, and never more so than in this sort of situation. If a horse leaps up in the air and comes down on your toe it can curtail your jumping ambitions for quite a time! You should also wear gloves; most people wear them whenever they lunge, which is sensible, but it is easy to become blasé and decide that the horse has always been so good you cannot be bothered to go and get them. That will almost certainly be the time that your horse does a Jekyll and Hyde and takes off round the school at 90 miles per hour, taking the skin off your fingers in the process.

Start on the left rein and walk towards the centre of the pole, which should be positioned so that the horse is walking towards the gate or the entrance: he is less likely to hesitate if he is heading towards home. Look ahead and do not hustle the horse, but use your voice to encourage him if he hesitates. Some will walk over it carefully, some pick up their front feet very neatly and forget all about their back ones, and some tap it with each foot in turn. The occasional horse decides that the pole must be treated with great caution and takes a great leap over it; all you can do then is try and keep out of the way, slip the lunge line so you do not end up being towed through the air and bring him back to walk as calmly as possible.

Occasionally you come across a horse who says that the pole on the ground looks very dangerous and he would rather not go anywhere near it. Keep cool and put

Horses who are suspicious of poles on the ground often gain confidence through this exercise. Start with two poles spaced wide apart, then gradually move them in until the horse walks over them.

another pole alongside it, with a gap about six feet between the two, and walk him between them. As he gets used to this, gradually narrow the gap until he is walking quietly over the two 'joined together' poles.

Another useful exercise – for any horse, not just the one who is worried about poles on the ground – is to lay four twelve foot jump poles on the ground in a square, with a gap at each corner big enough for the horse to walk through. Walk in one corner and out through the other, turn and walk over a pole, then over the one opposite, and so on at random. This gets the horse listening to your aids, looking where he is going, bending and using his shoulders. You should remember to look ahead (not down at the poles, or your weight will tip forward and you will encourage the horse to fall on his forehand) and to ride from the inside leg to the outside hand.

Whatever happens, do not make a fuss. Certainly do not scold him if he kicks the pole out; just repeat the process a few times until he seems happy and reasonably coordinated. Then change the rein and walk over the pole as before. Some horses will do this quite happily, whilst others hesitate slightly because things look different on a different rein. Horses have monocular vision – in simple terms, for most of the time they use one eye to look at things. Some people believe that this explains why a horse will go past a hazard, then spook at it when passing it from the other direction.

Lunge the horse over the pole in walk, then in trot, on both reins. Finish by putting a jump wing at the end and leading him over, then lungeing as before. There must be no risk of the lunge rein getting hooked up on the jump wings; some trainers use a sloping pole from the top of the wing, but a far better measure is to use a pair of plastic jump stands. These have no protuberances for the horse to knock himself against and are lightweight and easy to move about.

Start the next lesson by lungeing the horse, then walk and trot over a pole on the ground as before. By now he should be used to going over the pole with the school fence as a barrier down one side, so move the pole into the middle of the school and repeat the lesson. Add a second pole in a fan shape on the circle, so that the two are eight to nine feet apart at their centres; the distance allows for two trot strides, which are easier for the horse to cope with at first than one. This is where an observant helper is so useful, as he or she can move the poles if the distance is not quite right.

Once the horse can manage this on both reins, move the poles in so that they are four feet to four feet six inches apart on the circle. This will mean that the horse will take one stride; some people tell you that you should never use two trotting poles because the horse will try and jump them, but going from one pole to three is asking a bit much. If the horse trots through them at the two stride distance, he will inevitably do the same at the shorter one.

Finally, you can add a third trotting pole, again at the one stride distance. Coping with three in a row teaches the horse to coordinate his movements and pick up his feet – quite useful skills for jumping! The more poles you add, the more he has to concentrate.

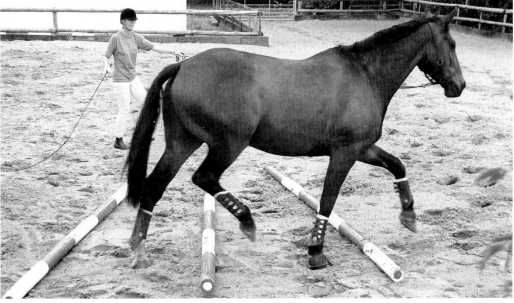

Poles placed on a fan mean the horse can be walked through the inside and trotted through the outside. They should be spaced according to your horse's stride length, but as a guide try three feet at the inside (for walk) and four feet six inches at the outside (for trot).

As he becomes more confident, you can raise the poles at alternate ends about six inches off the ground; this encourages the horse to flex his joints and pick up his feet.

As soon as your horse is coping confidently with poles on the ground, introduce him to his first jump. This is a simple cross pole, with the centre about one foot off the ground. The idea of the cross pole is that it encourages the horse to jump in the centre of the fence rather than to one side.

The box-of-poles exercise encourages the horse to use his hocks, place his inside hindleg underneath himself as he turns and concentrate on picking up his feet.

Some trainers like to put a ground pole about nine feet in front of the fence to encourage the horse to keep the rhythm of his trot and take off in the correct place. The trouble is that if he treads on the pole he may stop instead of taking off – and the last thing you want is to teach him how to refuse. A placing pole is useful later on, when he understands the idea of leaving the ground, but not right at the beginning.

Make sure he is settled and working in a nice rhythm on a circle, then introduce the fence. Do not hustle him into it, but make sure that you do not get in front of him as he approaches, as this will encourage him to slow down or stop. If he lands in canter, move forwards with him, put him on a canter circle that does not include the fence and bring him back to trot without any fuss.

Once the horse has negotiated a cross pole on its own, add a placing pole about nine feet away to encourage him to take off in the right place and make a round jump.

First fences under saddle

As soon as he has got the idea, he should start his jumping work under saddle. There is nothing to be gained by lungeing a horse over fences *ad infinitum*; loose schooling can be beneficial in that it gives the horse the freedom to sort himself out without a rider's weight affecting his balance, but lungeing makes him work in a smaller area. It is also very demanding of the handler in that you have to make sure you are in the right place, at the right time, when things are happening quite quickly.

Work him for five or ten minutes so that he is relaxed and listening to you, then start by walking over a pole on the ground, as you did with your lunge work. Keep a light contact; if the horse wobbles about or is reluctant to go forwards, open your hands to the side so that the contact remains, but is not a backwards pull. Once he is confident about walking and trotting over a single pole, add another eight to nine feet away so that he can take two trot strides between them.

Always work in rising trot, not sitting, as it is easier to stay in balance. Look ahead, not down at the poles, and allow the horse to stretch his head and neck as he goes over

Loose schooling allows the horse to jump without the hindrance of a rider's weight. You can also observe his technique – this horse is using himself in textbook style.

them. Your position should be just the same as for ordinary flatwork: do not try and assume any sort of 'jumping position' or you will simply throw the horse off balance and on to his forehand.

Shorten the distance between the poles so that there is room for a single stride, and concentrate on keeping the rhythm of your trot. If the horse shows a tendency to rush, set three poles on a circle in the same fan shape as before and three down the long side of the school. Work on a circle, then move off over the three in a row, keeping the same rhythm.

Remember that your bodyweight can have a marked effect on the horse's stride. If he tends to rush, sit more upright and slow the rhythm of your rising so that he rebalances himself to 'catch up'. Right from the start, you should establish that poles are nothing to get excited about.

If he tries to speed up when working over them on the straight, circle in front of them a few times until he settles and even becomes slightly bored, and then quietly trot through the line. Keep him guessing: circle, then go through the poles, then circle two or three times, then go through the poles and so on. You want to keep him guessing so that he is waiting to find out where you are going to go next, not anticipating.

Another good exercise is to scatter poles at random in the school, on their own and between jump wings. Walk over one, then turn away and trot over another, then circle without going over any poles, then turn and go over another one...and so on. You should be thinking all the time about balance and rhythm, so that going over a pole is simply another trot stride. This work has the same benefits as the box exercise detailed earlier, and the rider should keep the same principles in mind. It is important that the horse goes forwards, but is not hustled out of his natural rhythm.

Now turn your pole on the ground into a small cross pole fence, as you did on the lunge. Approach in a balanced, rhythmic trot and make sure that the horse has the freedom of his head and neck as he takes off – assuming, that is, that he makes a proper little jump. Some horses, especially the big, scopey types, decide that the easiest way to cope with such a piddling little fence is just to make an exaggerated trot stride over it. To encourage a proper jump, make the cross pole slightly higher in the centre – but make sure the sides are not too steep.

If your horse makes a huge jump over his first fence or decides to practise vertical take-offs, the last thing you want is to catch him in the mouth. Do not alter your position as you approach the fence, but as he takes off, fold forwards from the hips and allow with your hands; if necessary, push them along the crest of his neck. Try and stay as still as possible as the horse lands, as a slightly nervous or spooky horse is sometimes worried by the rider's weight leaving the saddle and coming back into it. Coming down with a definite bump is asking for trouble!

He will inevitably land in canter, so let him take two or three strides before bringing him calmly back to trot. Do not worry if he lands on the wrong leg; at the moment he is trying to find his balance. Try and keep everything calm and matter of fact and do not be so amazed that you have reached the other side that you throw the reins at him and become a passenger. The landing is just as important as the approach: you want him to come back to you and go forwards in the same rhythm, not collapse in an uncoordinated heap. Occasionally a horse will be so pleased with himself that he throws a buck on landing, so make sure that you are not sitting in such an exaggerated forward position that you are fired into orbit.

Once he has trotted over the cross pole on each rein, add a placing pole on the ground eight to nine feet in front of it, depending on the length of his stride. This will encourage him to take off in the right place and make a nice round shape over the fence. This done, call it a day and – as always – finish the lesson on a good note.

Many trainers use a placing pole right from the start. As previously pointed out, the possible drawback to this is that the horse who has never left the ground may trip over it and stop rather than carrying on an negotiating the cross pole – and the last thing you want him to do is realise that he can stop. Instilling the idea of getting up in the air first, then adding a placing pole obviates this risk.

This sequence shows how fillers are introduced. They are placed first as wings and then gradually moved in. The horse is the ex-racehorse shown in Chapter 13 and this was the first time she had been asked to jump through a grid.

For the next three or four days, give him a 10-minute jumping session incorporated into your normal hacking and schooling – the continuity seems to help and most horses progress very quickly. If you then give him a break from jumping for a week, nine times out of ten you will be amazed at his confidence when you introduce it again. With many horses, it is almost as if they spend their break thinking about what they have learned.

Always start each lesson by recapping the work you have done before. This does not mean that you have to go right back to square one every time, but it is important that the horse is not thrown straight in at the deep end. By all means give him some challenges and surprises later on, but only when the basics are well enough established for him to cope confidently.

In the early stages, approach your fences in trot. It is easier to keep the horse balanced and gives you more time to make a good approach. As soon as he is confident with the cross pole, build an upright fence about 18 inches high with a pole on the ground about six inches in front. The pole on the ground helps him judge when to take off; a single pole without a groundline is a difficult fence.

Although the vertical fence is no more difficult than his cross pole, it will look different. Keep the same active, rhythmic trot on your approach, with your legs round his side ready to push him quietly on if he starts backing off. The fence is deliberately kept small so that he can jump it from a standstill, if necessary – you do not want him learning that he can stop.

Jump on both reins equally, accepting that – as with his flatwork – he may find it easier on one rein than the other. Get your assistant to put another pair of wings just behind the first and change your vertical fence to a cross pole with a vertical pole behind it. This is his first spread fence, albeit a narrow one; the cross pole encourages him to jump in the centre. Finally, you can make the fence into a two foot spread with two vertical poles, the back one a couple of holes higher than the front one so he can see them both clearly. True parallels are more difficult for the horse to judge so should again be left until he is more experienced.

First doubles and new fences

The most important thing about introducing a horse to two fences in a row is to ensure that he knows they are there. That might sound silly, but some horses confronted with their first double will either go through the first fence because they are concentrating on the second one, or jump the first and stop in surprise at the second. To lessen the risk of this happening, set up two pairs of wings 18 to 20 feet apart, depending on the length of your horse's stride, with a pole on the ground nine feet before the first pair, a pole on the ground between them and a cross pole on the second. If you are using jump cups, always take them off wings that are standing empty and put them where the horse cannot hit them or land on them.

Trot over the poles and keep the same rhythm into the cross pole. Next, get your assistant to change the pole on the ground into a cross pole and approach in exactly the same way. The distance makes it easy and natural for the horse to pop over the first fence, take one canter stride and pop out over the second. Your job is to stay in balance and keep your legs round his side, ready to push him on if despite your preparations, he spooks at the second jump. If you are wrapped round his neck like a monkey up a pole, which some people imagine passes for 'The Jumping Position', you will put the horse on to his forehand and be in no position to influence him.

Soon two fences will be as easy as one, and you can start ringing the changes. Make the second fence into a cross pole with an upright behind, or a vertical with a pole on the ground six inches in front. The second fence must always be the same height or slightly higher than the first; never make the first fence higher, or the horse will dive over the second one instead of staying in balance.

At this stage, do not build your fences any higher than two feet – if things go wrong, the horse can step over them even if he is a bit close or too far away. It is bound to happen one day, and it is important that he learns to sort himself out right from the start. You should not attempt to place the horse, but should let him find his own way through these exercises: they have been built to make it easy for him and to give him confidence.

By now the horse will be used to jumping different arrangements of poles and can be introduced to solid looking fences. A lot of people worry about introducing their horses to brightly coloured fillers, but if done correctly there is no reason why they should cause problems. The best time to introduce them is at the end of a short jumping session, when the horse has jumped freely and happily.

Go back to a single fence: build a small vertical, about 18 inches high with a pole on the ground six inches in front. Bring in your fillers, but use them as wings – so that although they may look a little spooky, the actual fence is one the horse has jumped many times before. Approach in trot, and if the horse backs off encourage him with your voice and firm leg aids. If everything feels distinctly wobbly, open your hands to the sides so that you keep the contact, but there is no backwards pull.

Chances are the horse will take no notice of the filler wings at all, so as soon as he is confident, move them in slightly so that he is still jumping between them. It is then a simple process of gradually moving them closer together so that eventually he is jumping the fillers with a single pole on top. Do not jump the fillers alone; if he taps the pole it will roll, but if he knocks over one of the fillers he could trip over it and frighten himself.

You can use a similar approach with brightly coloured barrels, which must be anchored between poles so that they do not roll out and cause a fall. Build your single rail fence and put a barrel underneath at each end so the horse jumps between them. Gradually fill in the gap with more barrels until he is jumping the solid fence.

Try and get the horse used to as many different looking jumps as possible, all at 18 inches to two feet high. Planks, straw bales with a rail on top and barrel fences are all easy enough to make at home. They do not have to be show ring smart, just as bright as possible. Incorporate them into your little double, but always make the 'spooky' fence the first jump – if you put up plain rails followed by a filler fence, the horse may go through the first one because he is too busy looking at the second.

You can now build yourself a small, easy course to jump from trot, incorporating a change of rein and a one-stride double. Allow yourself plenty of room so that you can trot a circle and rebalance if necessary – if the horse lands over a jump and goes into canter, let him, coming back to trot at the next corner.

When he gives you the feeling that he is finding all this quite easy, he is ready to canter into a fence. Go back to your early grid and build your basic double down one long side of the school and an inviting single fence – such as a cross pole with a vertical one behind, about 18 inches high – halfway down the next long side. With luck, your horse will land on the correct leg through the double and you can keep the rhythm of the canter round the short side and into the fence. Do not try and place the horse; if the canter stride has a good rhythm, the fence will come to you. If he lands on the wrong leg, come back to trot in the corner, circle and establish the correct canter lead and approach the single fence as before.

Soon you will be able to jump your little courses in a mixture of trot and canter. Approach the first fence in trot and it should be no problem for the horse to land, go into canter and take the next fence in the same pace. When you need to change leg, come back to trot in the corner before the fence and ask for the new lead coming out of it. If you have so much room before the next fence that you can turn the horse on to a circle, come back to trot and correct the strike-off without the horse realising that he was heading for a jump, do so. If not, ignore the fact that he is on the wrong leg and come back to trot at a suitable point after the fence – never pull him away from a fence when you have started the approach, except in a dire emergency, or you are showing him how to run out.

Loose schooling

Loose schooling enables you to work the horse without any impediments or restrictions. It can be a very good refresher for an older horse as well as providing experience for the younger one, provided it is done well. Loose schooling should not be a euphemism for a horse careering round whilst the handler stands watching hopelessly; nor should it mean chasing him round with a lunge whip.

Proper jumping lanes, fenced 'alleyways' with jumps where the horse would be loosed at one end and jump down to the other, used to be part of every training yard's facilities. Nowadays they are much less common, probably because fewer people have the space available for them. Loose schooling in your ordinary work area is fine, as long as it is properly fenced and not too large.

The horse should wear a headcollar and be equipped with boots all round. The handler needs to be observant and active, as your position in relation to the horse will influence his speed and direction (at least in theory!) If the loose schooling area is small enough, you should be able to follow the same principles as if you were lungeing: stay slightly behind the girth with the lunge whip pointing downwards to drive him on, and move so that you are slightly in front of him, with the lunge whip raised, to slow him down.

If you want to loose school in a larger area, you will need an assistant to help keep the horse out on the track. Trotting poles and jumps should be set down a side of the school to make steering the loose horse easier; with you on one side of him and the fence acting as a barrier on the other, the risk of him ducking out to one side is minimised.

Chapter 9
Progressive Schooling

As your horse's education progresses, you will find that flatwork, jumping and hacking out complement each other; one will improve the other in a way that could never be obtained by working in a school day after day. Hacking out helps teach the horse to go forwards and listen to his rider despite outside distractions (even if he does seem rather deaf at times!) whilst jumping helps develop his ability to work from behind. Notice how, for instance, the first few strides of canter when he lands over a small fence are so often of a much higher quality, because of the extra impulsion.

Impulsion does not usually come naturally to the young, just broken horse when he is under saddle – though you may well see him exhibiting plenty of it when he is loose in the field. Lengthened strides, collection and even sometimes movements such as piaffe and passage are natural and effortless for the loose horse. Any horse or pony can move with grace, power and elegance (within, of course, the limitations of its conformation and paces.) If he can do it on his own, then he can do it with a rider as long as he is schooled and ridden correctly.

For most riders, the immediate aim is to get the horse 'on the bit', and they talk about it and work towards it as if it was a sort of Holy Grail. But it is a gradual process, not a case of learning to press the right magic button. The horse will not learn overnight to go on the bit and stay there for evermore; rather he will come into balance for a few strides at a time until he learns to carry himself. It is also important that the rider knows what it feels like to ride a well-schooled horse who is on the bit – no amount of description works unless you know what you are aiming for.

The horse who is on the bit is active behind and light in front. His engine, or driving force, is in his hindlegs and quarters and he accepts the bit with a light, flexible contact from the rider's hand. Think of this picture of perfection as a triangle ; one side is forward momentum, the second is establishing and maintaining balance and the third is the horse's acceptance of the bit and relaxation of his jaw.

Getting a horse so he works happily and consistently on the bit involves a series of stepping stones, of which perhaps the most important is the half halt. A lot of people find this a hard concept to understand, but a half halt is simply a way of asking the horse to rebalance himself. It is also a way of signalling to him that he is going to do something different, whether it be changing from one pace to another or changing direction.

In its most refined form, the half halt is a split second, barely perceptible rebalancing.

Introduce the concept by going forwards from walk to halt, then moving forwards after a couple of seconds. Gradually decrease the time spent in halt until you are not really halting at all, just pausing and moving forwards again. One word of warning, though: do not get so enthusiastic about this that the horse forgets how to halt and assumes that you move off straight away every time. Intersperse half halts with ordinary halts so the horse listens rather than anticipates.

Think of a half halt as riding up to a closed door that opens just as you get to it. Sit up straight, close your legs round the horse's side and your fingers round the reins. A split second before the horse halts, open your fingers and go forwards again. This has the effect of centring the horse's balance, putting his hindlegs underneath him and lightening the forehand.

This is one of the most useful things you can teach your horse and should be used whatever pace you are working in. Any time he runs on, loses his balance, falls on to his forehand, leans on the bit or whatever, use the half halt to rebalance him. It is not surprising that the half halt has been described as the aspirin of riding – if something goes wrong, use one!

The rein contact when a horse is working on the bit should be light and flexible, but the definition of that varies according to the horse's stage of training and the rider's preference. A horse working at advanced level can be working through from behind but still feel quite 'strong' in the rider's hands – though strong should not mean leaning or pulling. This is because he is generating an enormous amount of energy that has to be contained by the rider.

Some riders like their horses to feel light in the hand, whereas others prefer a more pronounced contact. As long as you are not conning yourself – in other words, that you are sure that the horse is neither letting you hold him up or tucking his nose in to avoid the contact – it is up to you to show him what is acceptable to you.

You cannot ask a horse to come on to the bit, and stay there, simply by wiggling the reins or trying to force his head and neck into a round outline. All that will do is prompt him to set his jaw against your hand and/or throw up his head and stiffen through his back. However, nor can you achieve the desired result by using your legs and seat and keeping your hands and arms motionless. You are asking the horse to push forwards, relax his jaw and carry himself and you in balance – so the communication has to be more subtle.

Some trainers believe that you should only start to ask with the reins when the horse is in trot, so that the forward movement is established first and there is less risk of shortening the walk stride. However, if you begin by asking the horse to flex his jaw in halt, he is halfway to understanding what you mean when you are asking him to do the same on the move. Take up the reins so that you have a light feel, then gently ask with the fourth finger of each hand. The movement should be little more than a vibration; it should merely encourage the horse to relax his jaw, not move the bit from side to side in his mouth.

As soon as he gives to you, *stop asking* and keep your light contact steady for a couple of seconds. Then give him a completely loose rein and pat him. If you carry on asking, he will wonder what on earth you want and will start fussing or tossing his head about.

With most horses, all this is far easier if he is ridden in a loose ring snaffle with either a single-jointed or French link mouthpiece. This is because the loose rings naturally allow a certain amount of play and it takes only very slight vibration of the rider's fingers to produce sufficient movement. If the horse has sensitive skin at the side of his mouth, fit rubber bitguards. An eggbutt snaffle or one of the other 'fixed' type of mouthpieces is not as subtle as a loose ring – though having said that, may be preferable if your horse is reluctant to accept a light feel on the bit and tries to come behind it all the time.

Once the horse has got the idea, get him walking forward freely and then ask him to relax his jaw in the same way, using the inside rein only. Once he does, just two or three strides are enough; reward him by offering him a loose rein, then ask again. Ask for the same thing in the same way in trot, being content with just a few strides at a time to start with.

No matter what the outline of his head and neck, and no matter how soft and relaxed the feeling of his jaw, he is not yet on the bit; all he has done is learn part of the equation. It is the use of half halts which puts it all together, the moments of rebalancing which allow the horse to gather himself together.

The horse is already used to the half halt as an instruction which means 'We're going to do something different', whether it be moving forwards from one pace to another or changing direction. By half halting within a pace, you ask him to put his hindlegs underneath him; by asking with a little vibration of the rein as you move forwards again you ask him to step forwards into a soft, relaxed rein contact. A lot is written and said about 'elastic' rein contact – when all the pieces of the above jigsaw fall into place, that is what you and the horse will have between you.

When you watch expert riders working their horses on the bit, it looks as if they are doing nothing but sitting there looking elegant. It is this which probably gives rise to the fond misconception that you get a horse on the bit and then do nothing but sit there and congratulate yourself. In fact, those expert riders are making a continuous series of tiny adjustments. For instance, if they feel the horse is about to come above the bit they rebalance with an imperceptible half halt, ask him to move on and move the bit slightly in his mouth so he cannot set himself against it. The communication between horse and rider is fluid, not static – it is a continuous conversation, not a 'Do this; thank you' followed by silence.

Moving away from the leg

In the early stages, your horse will have quite enough to do learning that when your legs close round his sides, it means go forwards. Now you can introduce the concept of moving away from the leg, not so that you can do all sorts of twiddly bits to impress people but so that your horse is more manoeuvrable.

The idea will probably have been introduced a long time ago, when the horse was taught to move over in his stable by holding his headcollar, nudging with the hand on the girth area and using the command 'Over'. If you bought him backed but lacking such refined stable manners, start in the same way.

This process can be taken a stage further by teaching him the turn on the forehand (which perhaps should really be called the turn around the forehand, as the last thing we want is for him to be actually on the forehand!) You need an assistant to help you in the early stages; ride the horse in the school as usual, and at the end of the lesson come to a halt facing the fence or wall so there is no risk of him banging into it. You will be turning him towards the entrance, which he will naturally be more receptive to.

The first stage of teaching a horse to move away from the leg: turn on the forehand, with a helper on the ground.

Your reins should be short enough to signal that you do not want him to move off, but you should not pull back at all. If you are turning to the left (in other words, if his head is moving to the left and his back end to the right) ask for a very slight bend to the left; this should be no more than a gentle feel on the rein.

Hold your right leg on the girth and put your left leg slightly behind it. Nudge with your left leg whilst your assistant presses her hand there and gives the command 'Over'. Only ask for one step at a time; you do not want the horse whizzing round in uncontrolled circles. Going slowly, a step at a time, allows you to keep the horse calm. If he is confused and tries to move off, gently stop him with the right rein; if he tries to step backward, close both legs round his sides to signal that you do not want him to do this. When he has settled, try again.

Once he has got the idea – and most horses pick it up pretty quickly – try the same on the other rein. You can now start by putting him parallel to the fence, about three metres away, and gradually ask for more steps round until you can manage a complete half turn; his quarters should move round the foreleg on the side to which he is turning and the inside leg should cross in front of the outside one. So if he makes a turn on the forehand to the right, his right foreleg is the pivot and his right hindleg crosses in front of the left one.

The classic reason for teaching the turn on the forehand is so that you can open gates from the saddle. However, it is generally used more often to manoeuvre in a tight space.

Leg yielding is even more useful in that it combines moving forwards and sideways with the horse's head bent slightly away from the direction in which he is going – so if he moves to the left, his head and neck are flexed very slightly to the right. Both front and hindlegs cross, the inside legs going in front of the outside ones.

Some dressage trainers do not like leg yielding, because they say it contradicts the half pass, when the horse bends in the direction in which he is moving. However, leg yielding is a much more natural movement for the horse: watch a horse shy away from something and he will bend his head and neck towards it and move away from it. It is also a very good suppling exercise, because the horse's inside leg steps underneath him, giving more spring.

Introduce it by turning down the three quarter line of your school or working area in walk, towards the entrance. Both the fence and the entrance act as a magnet; the horse will instinctively move towards them. If you are on the right rein, keep a slight flexion to the right, supporting with the left rein (which controls the speed and prevents his shoulders falling out). Half halt, then gently nudge very slightly behind the girth with your right leg to ask the horse to move forwards and sideways. Your left leg keeps the impulsion and stops the quarters swinging over too far.

As with anything new, practice and if necessary refine your technique on a schooled horse before trying to teach a youngster. When you do, only ask for a couple of steps to start with, then ride straight and forwards. As with turn on the forehand, do not practice leg yielding too often or the horse will start doing it when you have not asked him to.

Shoulder-in is another useful lesson that can be put to practical use; this exercise gives you control of the horse's shoulders, which in turn makes keeping him straight much easier. It is also a very effective way of riding a horse past a spooky hazard; put

Introducing leg yielding: the horse will naturally want to move back to the track.

him in shoulder-in so that he is looking away from the plastic bag in the hedge, or whatever, and he will usually go past it with much less trouble.

In shoulder-in, the horse's shoulders are brought off the track to the inside whilst his hindlegs stay on it. He bends to the inside and looks away from the direction he is going; his inside foreleg crosses the outside one, and his inside hindleg is placed well underneath him. The best way to introduce it is to ride a 10-metre circle in walk in the corner, just before the long side of your school. He must be going forwards, from the inside leg to the outside hand.

Starting shoulder-in. At the split second this photograph was taken, the horse dropped his shoulder and tipped the rider's weight slightly to the inside.

As you come on to the track, bring your outside hand to the neck and open your inside hand slightly, so you are moving the horse's forehand off the track. Your inside leg keeps him moving forwards, your outside one stops his quarters swinging out if necessary – and you look ahead, not to one side. At first, be satisfied with a couple of steps. As the horse gets the idea, ask for a little more: but always bear in mind that he must be moving forwards. Ride straight and forwards into trot, then forwards to walk again. As soon as you are confident that he understands you, ask for the same thing in trot.

More advanced jumping

Your horse should now be ready to tackle more advanced jumping exercises, to help make him more athletic. It will also give you the chance to see if his talents lie in this direction: whilst it is important not to overface a young horse, he needs to be asked a question or two. A well-known show jumping trainer once said that 'If a horse can't get a bit of height and spread as a four-year-old, he never will.'

Not everyone wants to jump enormous fences, and not every horse has the ability. But every horse should be able to jump three feet six inches if it is schooled and ridden correctly. Gridwork is the best and fairest way to start asking questions, because the fences are placed at distances which makes it easy for the horse (and rider!) to take off in the right place. Jumping a three feet six inch fence at the end of a grid is in many ways easier than cantering down to a three foot fence set on its own.

Grids can also be used to help improve a horse's technique. For instance, a grid of uprights will help improve the horse who dangles his front legs, whilst spread fences help the horse who is untidy behind. You must have a helper whilst you are doing this sort of work, as having to get off and move poles about is time consuming and breaks the continuity

All the distances given here are approximate and it is important that they are adjusted to suit your horse's stride. Eventually he will have to learn to cope with courses built round a standard canter stride of 12 feet, but make it easy for him in the early stages. If he is short striding, shorten the distances between fences by a few inches; if he is long striding, pull them out slightly.

As a rough guide, when a grid is approached in trot one non-jumping stride will be 18 to 21 feet and two non-jumping strides will be 32 to 36 feet. When a grid is approached from canter, the distances will be 24 to 26 feet and 34 to 36 feet. It cannot be emphasised too much that the distances must suit the horse's stride.

Remember that it is your job to get the horse to the fence and the horse's job to jump it. Do not try and place him coming in: aim to approach on a rhythmic, forward going stride without rushing. Your legs should be round the horse's sides to maintain impulsion and the rein contact should be light.

Gridwork gives horse and rider confidence, since if the approach and distances are correct the horse is automatically in the right place to take off. This horse dishes on his near fore and gridwork helps correct his tendency to drift to the left through combinations.

Start with a basic grid to be approached in trot: a pole on the ground, eight to nine feet in front of a cross pole, followed by a pole on the ground nine feet away, and a small spread fence nine feet away from that. The pole on the ground between the two fences helps keep the single canter stride between the cross pole and the spread round and bouncy. It also helps keep the horse in a round shape, as he tends to look at it.

The horse who tends to jump flat and dangle his front legs can be helped by building the following grid: a pole eight or nine feet in front of a small upright, followed by another pole nine feet away, with an upright nine feet away from that, then another pole and a third upright at the same distances. Make it more difficult by turning the middle element into a small ascending parallel, so that the horse has to open out but come back together for the final upright.

Bounce fences encourage the horse to bring his hocks well underneath him, but should only be used occasionally, to make the horse think. The event horse has to cope with bounces as part of his cross-country education; they help teach the show jumper and all-round horse to be athletic, too, but inevitably put more strain on the horse than a one-stride double. There is also the danger that if they are ridden too often, the horse may go into the aforesaid one-stride double and decide to try and bounce it, instead.

Introduce a bounce by incorporating it within a grid, to be approached from trot. A pole on the ground, nine feet in front of a cross pole, is followed by another pole on the ground and a cross pole at the same distances. The final bounce element is a third cross pole ten to eleven feet from the second.

Lots of books will advise you that you should jump small logs and ditches as part of your normal hacking out, behind a reliable schoolmaster at first to give your young horse confidence. If you are lucky enough to live somewhere that makes this possible, make the most of it – if not, find a well-built cross-country schooling course with lots of small fences and go with your escort horse.

Going somewhere different will be quite exciting for your young horse, so hack him round quietly until he settles. Your first cross-country fences should be no more than two feet high and should be approached from trot: small logs with good take-offs and landings are ideal. Once the horse is confident you can move on to slightly spookier fences; his show jumping training will have taught him that different fences are nothing to worry about, so ride with the same attitude, keeping your approach slow but with plenty of impulsion.

His first ditches should be small enough so that he can step over them, and the take-off and landing must be good. Slippery going will lead to a lack of confidence, so do not risk it. If possible, start over ditches with a low pole over the top so he gets up in the air. As always, approach in trot – and remember to look ahead, not down in the ditch, or you might end up in it!

If you have been able to ride through water out hacking, it should present no problems. If not, pick a water jump that is shallow with an even, firm bottom: get a helper to walk through it first to test it. Horses who worry about water do so not because they are frightened of the water itself, but because they cannot see where you are asking them to put their feet.

Walk in calmly behind your escort, stop in the middle and let him get used to it and walk out just as calmly. Be prepared for the horse who suddenly decides he would like to get out quickly and makes an enormous leap. Repeat the process, then stand the schoolmaster on the far side and ask the young horse to walk through towards him. Finally, he should walk through alone.

It is a good idea to jump your horse two or three times a week. Sometimes it can form the main part of his work, at others it can be just a 'little pop' after his flatwork or hack. At the moment he needs practice: older, established horses who are jumping regularly in competition do not need so much jumping at home unless you are trying to solve a problem.

Out and about

By now your horse should be hacking out confidently alone and with companions. Try and give him plenty of variety, so that he builds up a wide repertoire of sights and sounds. You need to be relaxed but not sloppy in your riding style – advice that is applicable whatever the age and temperament of the horse you are riding, but especially so with youngsters. Too many people become blase with quiet horses, slop along on a loose rein and then wonder why they end up on their backsides when the horse is startled by something. There is no such thing as a bombproof horse or pony, whatever the advertisements in the 'For Sale' columns would have you believe!

If you have hills to ride up and down, it will help get the horse fit. You need to adjust your balance to help him; sit slightly forwards so that your centre of gravity is in the correct place. When you are riding uphill, your weight should be slightly out of the saddle as if you were just about to take off over a jump. When you are going downhill, sit as if you had just landed over your fence. Keep a light contact and ride straight, not at an angle, so there is no danger of the horse losing his balance.

There are two schools of thought about hacking out. One looks on it as almost 'time off' for the horse, and believes he should be allowed to relax and forget about schoolwork. The other says that whenever he is being ridden, he should go nicely and listen to his rider. The second has a lot more to recommend it in terms of safety and fairness to the horse. If he only listens to his rider in a school environment, how on earth are you going to cope when you go to a show or take him hunting or on a sponsored ride?

The horse need not be on the bit all the time you are hacking out, but he should be what racehorse trainers call 'up to the bridle' – working from behind into a light, flexible contact. He should move off or away from the leg as soon as he is asked, not when he wakes up or has finished looking at whatever is so fascinating in the distance.

The mature four-year-old will soon get to the stage where he can cope with being worked every or nearly every day. Many people like to give their horses (or themselves!) a day off in the week; some horses take longer to settle back into work after they have had a rest day, whilst others pick up and carry on as normal. Keep him interested by keeping the work varied: hacking, schooling, jumping and lungeing and/or loose schooling all have their parts to play.

As soon as he is working confidently, take him to his first show. Think of this as being for experience only; forget about competing until he has been on a couple of outings. This applies even if he has been shown in-hand as a youngster, as you will still be asking him to concentrate on you to a much greater extent.

However mature and well behaved your horse is, he will find the distractions of a showground very exciting. Try and find one that is small but well-run and take a back-up party with you – a helper with plenty of common sense and an experienced horse who knows what it is all about. The idea is to get him used to the sights and sounds, not blow his mind.

Aim to arrive early, before things start hotting up. It is vital that your horse has as relaxed a journey as possible, so allow plenty of time and make sure his travelling equipment fits well and is therefore comfortable. Remember to travel him in a leather headcollar, or one of the new webbing kind with breakable rings. If anything goes wrong and he panics, the headcollar will break – but if you use an ordinary nylon one, his neck could go first.

Big horses, or those who are inclined to throw up their heads, should be fitted with poll guards. If you use the type with earholes, make sure they are large enough. Take the scissors to them if necessary, because if the pollguard pinches the base of the horse's ears he will throw his head about and be generally irritated. Little but important things like this sometimes go unnoticed, but if the horse associates standing in a horsebox or trailer with being uncomfortable, he may soon decide he does not want to load.

Some people opt for travelling boots rather than bandages on a young horse, because they are quicker and easier to take off. The trouble is that whilst there are some very good designs on the market, there are also some not so good ones. If the boots slip, the horse's legs are obviously not protected properly.

It is often better to use travelling bandages (as always, over padding) which are likely to stay in place better. If you tape over the fastenings, making sure that the tape is no tighter than the bandage itself, you can leave the bandages on whilst you work in. Not only do they provide excellent protection, they also mean that you can get the horse unloaded and working in without any hanging about. Once the horse has settled, you can take them off if necessary.

The horse's dock must be protected with a tail bandage or padded tailguard. If yours is one of those who likes to 'sit back' on the vehicle, put on a tail bandage, put bandage padding on the top and a second tail bandage over that.

If the horse comes off the ramp looking interested but fairly calm, you can get on him straight away. If he looks more like a fire-breathing dragon than a horse and you have the distinct impression that explosion point is not far away, lunge him for a few minutes first – if only for the sake of self preservation!

Find a corner of the showground where you will not get in competitors' way. Steer clear of the collecting rings; it is not fair to take up much needed space and the presence of horses being cantered and jumped nearby will only add to the excitement. The horse must be under control, which means lungeing off the bit rather than a headcollar or cavesson. Purists may frown at this, but the first two are not a lot of use if the horse decides to go faster and/or in the other direction from the one you had in mind.

Do not lunge him for hours on end, as this will tire him out. Although that may seem like a good idea when he is leaping in the air around you, he must be alert enough to listen to you when you actually get on him. All you need to do is work off his initial excitement.

Stick to a quiet spot when you start riding, using your escort horse as a calming influence. Keep your youngster going forwards and get him listening to you right from the start: this does not mean asking him to come on to the bit from the word go, but nor does it mean wandering around on a loose rein so that he is left to his own devices. There will be lots of things to distract him, but he should still stop and start when you ask him to, and it must be you, rather than him, who dictates the pace.

With young horses, you need eyes in the back of your head and a sixth sense that tells you when someone is going to dash past you or fire a horse over a practice fence from a standstill. A lot of people concentrate so hard on their own horse, or get so keyed up

Once your young horse has settled at a show, ride him round and show him the sights. This four-year-old later competed in – and won – his first novice show hunter class.

about competing, that they forget to consider everyone else. Even if you are wearing a tabard advertising the fact that your horse is young and unpredictable, do not assume that people will give you extra courtesy. Some will, but a lot more will not!

As your horse becomes more attentive, ask him to work on his own for a little while. Show him some of the sights – take him past trade stands and ice cream vans and make him stand for a few minutes while you chat with a friend. Make allowances for the distractions, but insist that he remembers good manners.

After a couple of outings like this, your horse should be ready to start competing. Pick your competition with great care and be prepared to back out if you arrive to find, say, a course that is on unsuitable going. Prelim dressage competitions are useful even if you intend to show jump or show: after all, you only have to walk, trot and canter! Do not worry if the horse is spookier and feels more tense than he is at home: as he gets used to going to different places, he will become more accepting of strange surroundings.

For the show jumper or eventer, clear round jumping competitions are useful as long

Working-in areas can soon get crowded. Try and find a space where your horse will settle.

as the course is well-built, with sufficiently substantial fences. Some shows run very good clear round rings and put as much thought and effort into them as they do with the main classes. Unfortunately there are others who build flimsy fences and cramped courses and stick them on an unsuitable site. If the fences and the ring are basically fine, but the course is too twisty for a novice, miss out a fence or two or alter the route to suit your horse. It is polite to explain your intentions to the steward before you go in, but no one will mind – after all, it is one less clear round rosette to give away!

The beauty of good clear round competitions is that show organisers realise that they are used for schooling purposes and will not (or should not) hustle you out the way if you hit a problem. If the clear round is not available, or is unsuitable, you will have to enter a mainstream novice class. Treat it as a schooling exercise – jump from trot whenever necessary, and if you achieve a clear round, ride the jump-off in exactly the same way. Riding against the clock comes later: at the moment your aim is a calm, balanced round.

Showing enthusiasts have to be prepared for the judge to ride their horse. This means getting him used to other people beforehand, both men and women. Ask proficient friends to have a sit on him at home, and pick your judge with as much care as you pick your show: the ideal is someone who is used to young horses and can be relied on to keep a sympathetic hand. Unfortunately not all judges come into that category: if you do not know him or her, find out from someone who does!

Chapter 10
Behavioural Problems

No matter how careful and correct you are in the way you handle and ride your young horse, there will be times when things do not go to plan. It may seem obvious to point out that horses are not machines, but it is all too easy to become frustrated when 'The Book' says that if you do X then Y will happen – and it appears that the horse has a different theory. Unless you have years of experience and have trained hundreds of horses (and therefore have learned by your own mistakes) you will hit the occasional setback.

Hopefully they will be minor ones that can be put right by working out where you went wrong and going back a step or two to put things right. Never make the mistake of ignoring minor problems in the hope that they will go away; it is much more likely that they will develop into bigger ones. The yearling who is allowed to nip because 'it's normal coltish behaviour' will grow up into the horse who bites because he has been allowed to express his dominance in this way – but the one who is shown from the start that this sort of behaviour is unacceptable will also have been shown that you are higher up in the pecking order than he is.

If at any stage in your horse's training you feel out of your depth, get help from an experienced person who is used to dealing with young horses. This book can point you in the right direction (and help you to stay on it) but there may be times when you need help in assessing your particular horse and situation. Obviously it is important to pick the right person: judge them by their horses' attitude and behaviour. Brutality should not be countenanced, but nor should the sentimental approach. Look for the right mixture of caring, common sense and experience.

You may also buy a young horse whose training was started by someone else and find that you have unwittingly bought problems along with him. They may or may not have been caused by the previous owner: every horse occasionally says 'I don't want to do that' or 'I don't understand'. It is only when he is allowed to dictate things or confusion is not cleared up that a glitch becomes an established problem.

This chapter and the next look at some of the common problems that arise with young horses and suggest some proven ways of solving them. It is still important, though, that you know your own horse so that you can adapt these methods accordingly. Is he a bold character who could easily become pushy? Or is he the cautious sort who must learn to have confidence in his rider? Horses, like people, have personalities – which are the result partly of their breeding and 'natural' temperament and partly of the way they are kept and brought up.

Opinions vary as to how intelligent horses are, but it is a mistake to judge their intelligence (or otherwise) in human terms. Even though they have been domesticated for about 5,000 years, they retain their natural instincts and characteristics. These can be used to work for you, but they can also work against you: some of the best trainers achieve their results because they 'think like a horse' rather than trying to apply human values and logic.

In the wild, horses are herd animals. They are also prey, as opposed to hunters: their natural defence is flight, and it is very rare that a horse will actually attack someone. He may nip or bite, and he may kick out if frightened, but that is usually as far as it goes.

Horses are herbivores designed to spend most of their time foraging and eating. Even then, instincts stay in place – watch a group of horses in a field and you will often see that if the majority lie down, one or two will remain standing 'on guard'. Horses do not naturally eat grain and they do not weave, crib bite or windsuck in the wild.

So-called stable vices are caused by the way horses are kept. In many ways, the best kept horse is the 'ordinary' pony who is kept out all the time. The ones who should be pitied most are the (usually valuable) animals who are kept stabled except when they are being exercised: it is no coincidence that the highest incidence of stable vices is amongst racehorses who are stabled for 22 or 23 hours out of every 24.

It would be naïve to suggest that every horse should be turned out all the time, but your young horse will benefit if he is kept as naturally as possible. By all means bring him in at night, but ride him 'off the field' and you will find him far more relaxed and amenable. Obviously he needs enough feed to enable him to grow and develop and to cope with the work he is being asked to do, but be careful not to overfeed.

All the time he is growing and learning, your horse is finding his position amongst his companions in the field – in other words, in the herd. He is experimenting to find who is superior to him and who is subservient, and there will be times when he tries to find out where he stands with you, too: as far as he is concerned, you are (or should be!) the herd leader.

A lot of people are surprised when the horse who was so meek and mild as a three-year-old suddenly goes through a phase, often as a four-year-old, of turning bossy or saying 'I won't'. You often hear the complaint that 'He used to be really good and now he's trying it on all the time'. That is exactly what he is doing – trying it on to see how far he can go. It is important to show him what the boundaries are and to keep them in place.

No horse is an angel on four legs. If it was, it would either be brain dead, boring or both. But setbacks are not necessarily yours or anyone else's fault: the horse who suddenly naps and decides that he does not want to leave the yard is seeing what he can get away with. Setbacks only become problems if they are allowed to go unchecked.

If you find you have to cope with a problem, always check the obvious (but often ignored) possibilities first. Does the horse have sharp edges on his teeth, wolf teeth, mouth ulcers or discomfort because he is cutting teeth or tushes? Wolf teeth, which are found in both mares and geldings, are best removed; tushes often cause a lot of discomfort when they are coming through, but then settle down.

Is his saddle, bridle or girth pinching him? One of the authors knows of a mare who was sold to a very caring home and suddenly became headshy: every time her owners tried to take off her bridle she threw up her head or even reared. The reason was that the browband on their new bridle was too small and pinched the base of her ears. It took a new browband and a lot of patience to get her back to normal – far longer than it took for the head shyness to develop.

No matter how nice the horse, sometimes he will say 'no'. Keep riding him forwards, because if he is going forwards he will find it harder to nap or buck.

The other moral of the above story is that horses have long memories. If a horse has an unpleasant experience, he will remember it, so you have to accept that it can take some time for a problem to go away even when the original cause has been removed.

The methods suggested in this book are not always orthodox, but they are all tried and tested! Whatever you do, safety must be paramount. This ranges from standing in the right place to wearing gloves, a hard hat and/or protective footwear when necessary. We all take risks that we know we should not sometimes, perhaps because we are in a hurry, but the day you lead your newly shod, lively three-year-old in from the field wearing canvas shoes because of the hot weather is the day he will choose to leap in the air and put one of his new shoes on your unprotected foot.

There are all sorts of ways of saying 'no'! Thirty seconds later this three-year-old was working quietly and happily again.

Again, safe handling comes down to remembering the horse's instincts. If something frightens him, he runs away from it – so when you introduce something new, whether it is putting on a roller or giving him his first clip, you and your helper should stand on the same side of the horse. If you stand on the nearside and your helper is on the offside,the horse who is worried or uneasy about the clippers or the roller is going to jump away from it – and probably land on your helper.

It may be necessary, for safety's sake, to use a suitable method of restraint and/or suitable equipment. If the horse has been bitted, a bridle gives far more control than an ordinary headcollar. There are designs intended to give you extra help, most of which work by tightening on the nose when the horse pulls and slackening again when he comes back. They can be useful on an unbitted, immature horse, but their effectiveness is limited on a more powerful one.

If you have to use a headcollar, clip a lead-rein to the offside, if you are working on the nearside. If you are working on the offside, clip it to the nearside. Pass it under the chin and and out through the other side of the headcollar so it acts like a curb chain. If the horse is big and stroppy, use a leading rein with a chain section near the clip. It can also be fastened in a similar fashion over the front of the nose, but this is more severe.

The 'curb chain technique' can be used with an ordinary snaffle bridle to give you more control over a horse which barges or pulls. If you are leading from the nearside, pass a leading rein or lunge line through the nearside bit ring, under the chin and clip it to the offside bit ring. Reverse this if leading from the offside.

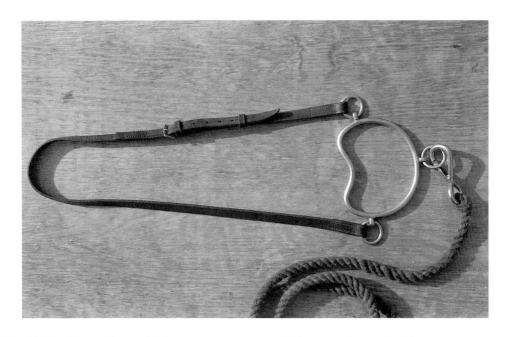

The Chifney bit can be useful for giving extra control, but must be used with care.

The Chifney bit, which encircles the lower jaw, gives maximum control over a horse that tries to rear and for this reason is often used when handling difficult colts. It should be used with care, because it is capable of exerting tremendous leverage on the bars of the mouth and the lower jaw – but if all else fails, it may be the safest choice. It is only used for leading a horse, never when riding him.

Correctly fitted Chifney bit.

You can sometimes distract a horse who is objecting to something by simply pinching a fold of skin on his neck. If this is not enough, the safest and most humane way to control him is to use a twitch on his top lip: never put it anywhere else. When applied correctly, a twitch does not hurt a horse. It is now known that it stimulates the production in the body of natural substances called endorphins, which are relaxants that produce a pleasurable sensation.

Handling problems

Barging and pulling
Barging is a sign of either ignorance or fear. The youngster who leaves his first home and is put into a strange stable will be understandably bewildered and may barge anyone who goes in with him because he is in 'fright and flight' mode. The last thing you should do is punish him; make sure his surroundings are as safe as possible, with other horses in constant sight, and let him settle.

The ignorant barger who literally throws his weight around is a different kettle of fish. If he barges as soon as you open the door, approach it with a short stick in your hand and bang the door. He will inevitably step back or at least stop still at the noise; if he barges at you again as you open it, say 'No' in a sharp tone of voice and give him a single sharp smack across the chest. Do not hit him any higher up, or you risk making him headshy.

If he barges or pulls while you are leading him, equip him as explained before. If he has been bitted, a snaffle with a lunge line or lead-rein and chain is the best bet. Hold the rein in your inside hand and carry your short stick in the other, and if he tries to rush off, use your voice and check him with a definite 'give and take' on the rein. Avoid setting up a steady pull, or you will simply set up a contest that he is bound to win.

If this is not enough, smack him across the chest as before whilst you scold him and give and take on the rein. As soon as he comes back to you and stops barging, praise him.

Nipping and biting
Watch youngsters turned out in the fields and you will often see them nip at each other in play as they try to gain supremacy – no wonder the phrases 'horseplay' and 'horsing around' found their way into the English language! But if yours tries to do the same to you, he must be shown in no uncertain terms that such behaviour is not on.

Nipping may well be 'coltish' but the most bumptious colt should learn that he does not behave like that with people. Bring out the short stick again, and if he bites you, tell him off and smack him across the chest. A slap on the nose is effective for a one-off offence of this kind, but if repeated is likely to make the horse headshy. He may also learn to bite, jump out of the way and/or throw up his head to avoid being smacked.

A horse will also bite if he is uncomfortable. Introduce grooming by starting with your hands, then moving to a soft brush – and if the horse is thin-skinned, as will be the case with well-bred animals, avoid using hard dandy brushes on him. Careless girthing up, by you or a previous owner, can also provoke a horse to bite. Do it carefully and pull the forelegs forward before mounting to ensure that there are no folds of skin trapped; horses soon learn to do this and will pick up their legs of their own accord.

If the habit is established, and the horse anticipates discomfort even when you are gentle, tie him up in the stable to groom, put rugs on and so on. When this is not possible, put on his bridle and take the reins over his head. Put the reins over to the opposite side from where you are working and pass them over the neck, back to your hand. If the horse attempts to bite, pull and release and say 'No' sharply.

Bridling

Youngsters who are headshy about having a bridle put on or taken off associate it with discomfort or simply do not want a piece of cold metal in their mouths. The solution is the same in both cases, once you have double checked that mouth problems are not to blame.

Use a headcollar that fastens at the nose and at the side and clip the leadrope on as usual. Put a saddle or roller on and fasten the leadrope so that it acts as a standing martingale – tight enough to stop the horse throwing his head above the angle of control, but not so tight that he feels so restricted that he panics. You should now have sufficient control to be able to put on the bridle very gently; make sure it fits comfortably and that nothing is pinching, then remove the headcollar.

This method is much safer than standing on something to give you extra height. The problem here is that if the horse throws his head up or barges you, you could end up in a heap on the stable floor.

Aggressive when feeding

Some youngsters show aggressive tendencies when they are fed, especially if they have been fed 'in the herd' in the field as weanlings and have had to learn to stand up for themselves and keep others away from their feed. But however understandable their behaviour, it must be stopped – being trapped in a stable by a stroppy horse protective of his feed is no fun!

Put his food at the front of the stable, not the back, so that you have a clear exit. If he will eat from it, use a door manger so that you do not have to go in at all. If you are putting food in a manger or putting a feeding bowl on the ground, carry a stick as you approach. If he goes for you, smack him across the chest and give a sharp 'No!' Praise him when he stops or shoots back; you want him to learn that when you open the door, he steps back to let you in.

Kicking

Any horse will kick out if something startles him from behind. But if he uses kicking as a form of aggression – i.e. as a protest against something he dislikes – he must be shown that this is against the rules.

Treat thin-skinned, sensitive horses with respect when grooming, girthing up, clipping etc. If kicking is a habit, anyone standing nearby must be out of range and anyone handling him must be close enough that he cannot get his leg up and back to lash out.

Stand to one side when grooming, putting on a tail bandage etc. Some horses dislike having their legs handled or brushed; if he has not been taught to accept this, treat him as if he was a foal and insist through repetition that he lets you run your hands over his limbs, starting with the front ones. When you are working round the danger area, pressing hard on the point of the hock prevents him drawing his leg up to kick.

A lot of horses are sensitive round the belly area and will cow kick when being groomed or clipped. Use the flat of your hand rather than a brush to remove dirt – and wear a hat or skull cap.

Loading

If a youngster is difficult to load – or a previously good traveller suddenly starts playing up – then 99 times out of 100 it is because he has had a bad experience. Double check the state of the vehicle, which should be light and inviting, and make sure that he has plenty of room to spread his legs and balance himself. Moving the partition in 'to give him some support' is usually the worst thing you can do; if you are using a two-horse trailer, you may have to take out the centre partition altogether.

Driving skills are vital. The keynotes, whether you are using a horsebox or a trailer, are smooth acceleration, braking and gear changes. Are you anticipating far enough ahead – for instance, are you slowing down for a roundabout in time?

You must give him confidence that it is safe to walk up the ramp. Look where you are going, never back at him, and if he stops, try not to turn away. Some horses worry about whether a ramp is safe; pick up a front foot, put it on the ramp and let the horse investigate. Do not tell him off if he paws the ramp, because this is his way of testing it for safety.

If you cannot encourage him in with a bucket of food, enlist two helpers and fasten a lunge line to each side of the vehicle. Each helper holds a line and stands to the side, out of the range of the horse's hindlegs. As he approaches the ramp they cross over behind, again out of range, so the lines cross over and put slight pressure on his back end. Be careful that they do not slip over his back or below his hocks.

If you still have problems, it is well worth hiring a good, professional transporter for half a day. Ask around for recommendations: you want someone who is used to young horses and can be guaranteed not to lose his or her temper.

Shoeing

Shoeing difficulties vary from the big, ignorant youngster who has not been taught to pick up his feet to the one who hates having the nails banged in and is determined to avoid it. The best person to help is a good farrier with an even temper who knows when to insist and when to go with the horse.

When you ask a young horse to pick up his foot, make sure he is properly balanced first and be content with a little at a time. Pick up the feet in the same order each time;

horses soon learn the routine and will pick up their feet for you. If he is an awkward customer who has learned that if you lean into his leg and shoulder, all he has to do is lean back, squeeze the chestnut on the leg you want him to lift. You have to squeeze hard – and be prepared for the leg to come up pretty smartly. As it does, take hold of the toe.

Although shoeing a horse obviously does not hurt him, some dislike the pressure as the nails go in. The only answer is time and familiarity; practice picking up his feet and banging them with a dandy brush.

Young horses get bored standing around. It is quite common for one to be reasonably well behaved at first and then start fidgeting. If he is worse with the back feet than the front ones, the farrier may decide to do these first; if the horse has good, strong feet it might be worth shoeing him just on the front for the first few times. You will not be doing hours of roadwork – and it lessens the risk of your horse damaging another if he kicks out in the field.

If the horse is so bad to shoe that he is dangerously unmanageable, you will have to ask your vet to sedate him. Hopefully he will realise that there is nothing to worry about and become more amenable.

Stable vices

Stable vices can often be lessened to a manageable degree, or even cured, by turning the horse out as much as possible. Crib biting and windsucking are the hardest to deal with, because often the horse will indulge his habit on any available surface. If he cribs on post and rail fencing, the best bet is to put electric fencing on the inside – though this may not be possible if you keep him at livery.

Foul tasting preparations painted on favourite cribbing spots, such as door ledges, deter most horses (though they may simply go off and find somewhere else.) There is also a roller toy which fits in the stable and is said to occupy some horses – they cannot set their teeth on it, so are unable to crib or windsuck on it.

A crib biting strap, with a metal arch which causes discomfort when the horse arches its neck to crib, is another classic deterrent. Most drastic of all is an operation in which a layer of muscle is shaved off the neck. It is designed to stop the horse arching his neck to crib, but does not stop him working on the bit and does not affect his appearance.

Chewing is not officially a vice, but can be equally annoying and expensive. Horses that are teething will often chew wood to try and relieve their discomfort; all you can do is paint cribbing deterrents on the woodwork. If the horse chews or tears at his rugs, check that he is not too hot and that the fabric is not making him itchy. Some horses with sensitive skin will settle if you put a cotton summer sheet under other rugs.

Youngsters investigate things with their lips. If you leave things within reach – rugs, reins, stable brooms etc – they will often pick them up and chew them. The answer is obvious: leave nothing within the horse's range!

Weaving is the commonest vice. The best way to stop it is to turn the horse out as much as possible and to keep him in a stall when he has to be in. Horses who weave like the proverbial tops in loose boxes will nearly always relax and stop the habit when they are put in a stall with other horses on either side. They need to be on a ball and rope so that they can get up and lie down safely.

If your horse gets on with his neighbour, you can often reduce or stop his weaving by taking down the top kicking boards between the two stables so that the horses can see each other and touch noses. Anti-weaving grids work in some cases, but not others; full grids turn a stable into a prison and all that happens is that the horse weaves behind it.

Some horses settle on a busy yard whereas others like peace and quiet. Some like radios playing, others retreat to get away from the noise. But give a horse as natural a lifestyle as possible and vices – which are manmade and a reaction to stress – will be minimised.

Chapter 11
Schooling Problems

Even the best riders occasionally get a communication breakdown. It happens to everyone, including professionals, and for all sorts of reasons. Horses, like people, are individuals. What one finds easy, another will find difficult – it may be due to conformation, it might be because of that particular horse's temperament, or it could be a combination of both. It may also be because you have not been consistent in your aids, or because you have been so encouraged by the horse's progress that you have tried to advance a stage farther before the previous one has been established.

There is a fine line between asking the right questions at the right time and being in too much of a hurry. Your horse's training is a bit like a pyramid: if the base is not secure, it will be unsteady. Equally, you can go too far the other way and be over cautious about moving on. Your horse does not need to be working perfectly on the bit before he tackles his first fence . . . but if you try and canter round a course before you can do the same on the flat, you will be in trouble.

Throughout your horse's education, you ask him to do things which he finds difficult or which he would not do of his own accord. He is a herd animal and likes to be with other horses, so why should going out of the yard on his own be enjoyable? He balances himself naturally by putting his head and neck to the outside, so of course he finds it harder to take an inside bend. Putting his hindlegs farther underneath his body and coming on to the bit is a feat of balance and athletic skill that takes time and preparation – is it surprising that he sometimes goes above or behind the bit because he loses coordination or the rider is out of balance?

This chapter looks at some of the common riding problems and how to cope with them. As has already been stressed (and cannot be repeated too often) *check the obvious first*. If your horse puts his head in the air because the bit is in contact with wolf teeth, no amount of transitions or experimenting with tack will put things right. If he is tense through his back because his saddle is uncomfortable, you will not get anywhere until the discomfort is removed.

Sometimes you will find that the use of a particular type of bit, noseband or training aid is suggested. Training aids, or gadgets as some people prefer to call them, are controversial and probably always will be – and for that reason have been dealt with in depth in the next chapter.

There are three facts which few trainers would argue with, though. One is that to ride and school horses successfully you need to keep an open mind and assess every animal as an individual – so condemning all training aids out of hand is a bit like insisting that the world is flat. The second is that in the right hands, used for short periods, they can sometimes achieve a breakthrough when all else has failed. The third is that in the wrong hands, they can make a problem worse . . . so the moral of this story is pretty obvious! If you think a chambon, draw reins or whatever would help you sort out a problem but are not sure how to use them, get help from someone who does and who has the results to prove it.

The schooling problems, like the handling ones, have been listed in alphabetical order for ease of reference. This is not a comprehensive guide to dealing with every equestrian drawback under the sun: there are plenty of complete books devoted to just that subject. As with handling problems, it is only possible to offer food for thought, guidelines and a few tried and tested methods. It is up to you to decide which may apply to your situation, bearing in mind your horse's temperament and your own capabilities.

If you have the slightest doubt that you have hit a snag you cannot work through alone, then once again the message is the same – get help! The longer a problem goes on, the harder it is to resolve.

Above the bit
When a horse is on the bit he is working from behind, into the rider's hand – accepting the bit, using his hocks and staying in balance. This is the aim everyone works towards, but it is a gradual process. The young or unschooled horse has to learn how to find and keep his balance, and if he finds it difficult will try and find an 'escape route' by coming above or going behind the bit.

The horse who comes above the bit will be stiff backed and not working through from behind correctly. His nose will come in front of the vertical and you will probably feel that you have little or no influence over the way he is going. This may happen only occasionally, usually when you ask him to readjust his balance and make a transition. In the very worst scenario, the horse will be above the bit all the time. When this happens, he may develop a ewe neck even if his conformation is not naturally that way inclined, as his carriage will build up muscles on the underside of the neck. If his natural conformation is ewe necked, he will only be able to work within the limits of it.

When you are sitting on a horse who is going with his head in the air and his nose poking out, it can seem tempting to try and redress the balance by using stronger rein aids. This only makes the situation worse and leads to the horse backing off: he needs to be ridden forwards and asked to do lots of transitions and half halts in order to get his hindlegs farther underneath him

If he comes above the bit in transitions, make sure you ask for a definite half halt before you ask for one so that he knows something different is coming. Make sure that he is not coming above the bit because your hands are restricting him or because you are sitting deeper or using stronger seat aids than his physical development can take.

Check, too, that you are not fixing your hands too low in an attempt to get him to lower his head.

A loose ring snaffle of some description is often the best bit for the horse who comes above the bit. Its construction means that it moves rather than stays still in the horse's mouth, and it is therefore harder for him to set himself above it. Fixed bits such as eggbutt or full cheek snaffles make it easier for him to evade by coming above the bit, so are usually unsuitable.

If the horse is an older animal who has become practised at this evasion, a training aid such as a chambon, draw reins or running reins can help to show him what you want. But before using anything like this, read the next chapter and note all the dire warnings!

Behind the bit

The horse who is behind the bit – who drops the contact and is usually not going forwards – must also be encouraged to work more from behind. Work him on a long rein with a light contact to start with and be extra careful to use the influence of your weight rather than your hands when you ride downwards transitions or half halts. Try opening both reins – moving both hands out to the side without pulling back at all – so that when you ride forwards, the horse has to work up to the bridle but there is no danger of him being pulled back.

This horse is usually happier with, and goes best in, the sort of bit which stays still in his mouth. Avoid the loose ring snaffle recommended for the horse which goes above the bit, and instead try an eggbutt or full cheek version. A mullen mouthed snaffle, without a joint, is sometimes accepted: Nathe snaffles, with their light, flexible mouthpieces, are excellent for persuading a horse to take a contact.

Once you have established his basic confidence in your hand through work on a long rein and, if necessary, a change of tack, you should be able to ask him to work within a shorter frame. Do not think just of shortening the reins: he must *always* work from the leg into the hand.

Canter strike-off

Most young horses get their canter strike-offs muddled up sometimes, either because they, their riders or both are unbalanced. The most obvious causes of wrong strike-offs are lack of preparation before asking for the transition, too strong an outside leg or a restricting outside rein. If the horse canters on the correct lead on the lunge, but not when ridden, there are no prizes for working out that rider error is to blame.

When you are schooling, only ask for a transition – any transition – when the horse is balanced and going forwards. As long as you have a slight bend to the inside and the horse is between hand and leg, you should get the correct strike-off. The word is 'should' rather than 'will', because there is always the odd horse who refuses to canter with a particular lead.

If the horse has not already been taught the shoulder-in movement, teach him. Ride him in shoulder-in as you trot round the corner of a short side of the schooling area, and stay in shoulder-in as you ask for canter coming out of the next corner. This is also a good way of explaining to the horse that you want him to strike off on a particular lead on the straight; as he grasps the idea, you will be able to refine your aids until he takes his cue from your weight distribution alone.

Awkward customers who do not respond to this can often be persuaded by the use of a small cross pole. It should be positioned about two thirds of the way down the diagonal of your schooling area and set just high enough for the horse to jump it rather than take a long trot stride. Approach in trot on the horse's 'difficult' rein and open the rein to the inside as he takes off. Be careful not to pull back or to drop your weight to the outside; if anything, there should be slightly more weight on the inside stirrup than the outside one. If he lands on the correct leg, stay in canter for a complete circuit; if he lands on the wrong leg, come quietly back to trot and try again.

Once he has got the idea with the cross pole, you may find that you have broken the barrier and have very few problems. If, however, you find you are back to square one, repeat the cross pole exercise and then replace the fence with a pole on the ground. Trot in as before and give the canter aids just as he is about to step over it.

Jumping

All horses can jump, though some are better at it and enjoy it more than others. Even the best, most courageous and athletic jumpers sometimes have problems and either send the poles flying or stop because they cannot sort out their legs. It is when poles hit the ground more often than they stay in the cups or stopping/running out threatens to become a habit that you have something to worry about.

If you have been working on your own, the best way to sort out jumping problems is to have a few sessions with an experienced jumping trainer who is used to working with young horses. He or she can assess both of you and take you back to basics to restore the horse's confidence. Stopping is nearly always down to lack of confidence, either caused by asking too much, too soon, or because the horse feels he is in the wrong place to take off. He may be reluctant to take off because you are unknowingly restricting him instead of freeing his head and neck as he takes off, or because his saddle pinches as his shoulders move, or simply because he does not feel like it and is trying you out . . . there is a whole range of possible causes, and a good eye on the ground is essential to pinpoint the appropriate one.

Running out, when the horse ducks to one side or the other, is usually sorted out with more effective riding. Most horses have a preference for the side they run out to, and it is often the left (perhaps because most horses are more supple on the left rein than the right.) Make sure you do not encourage the horse to run out through bad presentation: he must be put to his fences straight, not at an angle. (When you have solved the problem, by all means teach him to jump on an angle – but wait until his confidence is restored.)

To ride effectively in this situation, you must make sure you are not in front of the horse's movement. Avoid taking a 'jumping position' on the approach; instead, sit up straight and keep your legs round him. You only need to fold forwards from the hips when he actually takes off. If he tends to run out to one side more than the other, carry your stick down the shoulder on the side of his 'escape route' and if you feel he is about to duck out, give him a sharp tap down the shoulder and use your legs. This is one of the rare occasions when it is effective to use a stick on the shoulder rather than the girth, but timing is important: it is no good if it comes too late!

A change of tack can help with the horse who sticks his head in the air and/or opens his mouth and runs out to one side. A snaffle with full cheeks or D-rings gives more steering power if the horse goes well in it: if you use a loose ring snaffle and do not want to change it, rubber bitguards are sometimes surprisingly effective. A correctly fitted Flash noseband helps keep the bit central in the horse's mouth and may also help with your steering.

A martingale may also be helpful; either the universally popular running martingale or the unfashionable standing. Sometimes a standing martingale can be more effective; a lot of people worry about using them for jumping, but as long as it is not fitted too tightly it will not restrict the horse as he jumps. Watch a horse over a fence and you will see that his head and neck move forwards and downwards. If his head goes up, then of course the martingale will say 'No' – which is exactly what you want.

Some horses have a tendency to hang to one side or the other when they jump. In the worst extremes, they may hit a wing, with disastrous results. Correct riding coupled with gridwork will help – get someone to watch you riding and make sure that you are not inadvertently tipping to one side or the other, which will affect your horse's balance. Ride straight, look ahead and if the horse swings to one side, push both hands towards the ear on the opposite side. If he jumps to the left, push both hands towards his right ear. This is more effective than simply opening the rein.

It also helps to use guide poles on your fence in a V-shape; this encourages him to jump in the centre. Start by placing them far apart, then gradually bring them in until the horse is jumping over a tight V. This also helps horses who are not sharp enough with their front feet, as they have to pick them up higher to clear the fence.

Lazy horses

Most horses are not naturally forward going when they first start their education under saddle. After all, why should they be? They have to learn a whole new language – the rider's aids – and to go at the pace and in the direction they are asked to instead of moving around at their own volition. Your aids need to be definite but not prolonged or heavy. Always aim to start by using the lightest aid possible; if you get no reaction, stop and ask again, more definitely this time.

V-poles encourage a horse to jump in the centre of a fence and to pick up his foreleg.

Some horses are more energetic than others, but even those whose natural inclination is to take life in an easy style must learn to react to and go forwards from light aids. You see too many riders nagging at their horses, legs moving constantly at the horse's sides – and the result is that the horse switches off and becomes 'dead to the leg'. Rather than get into this habit, use a schooling whip to reinforce leg and voice aids.

This does not mean that you have to beat up your horse. In fact, the reverse is true: in the long run you will be making life a lot more comfortable for him than if you keep drumming away at his sides. Give a light but clear aid to move off, and if the horse does not respond immediately, give a sharp tap just behind the girth with the whip. Do not be satisfied with the horse who moves off two seconds after you give the aids: you want an instant reaction.

Click with your tongue at the same time as you tap him sharply with the whip, and make sure you allow with your hands. The horse is likely to jump forwards in surprise, and you do not want to catch him in the mouth so that in effect you are punishing him for obeying. Whether he jumps forwards or walks off smartly, give him a pat and a word of praise. It will not take long for the message to sink in. Soon you will be able to dispense with the whip aid, and then with the voice, except perhaps as occasional reminders.

Riding the lazy horse with blunt spurs (provided you can ride well enough to use them only when you want to) can often be effective. Do not use them every time you give an aid: only if the horse does not respond to the 'ordinary' leg.

Leaning on the bit

The horse who leans on the bit and wants you to hold up his head for him is invariably on his forehand and therefore not working from behind. It is important to use a bit that makes this difficult, so if you are using a 'fixed' snaffle such as an eggbutt, change it for a loose ring. A thinner mouthpiece is often more effective than a thicker one in this case – some horses go 'dead' with a thick bit and some simply dislike having a lot of bulk in their mouths. A loose ring bridoon (the thin snaffle which partners the Weymouth in a double bridle) is accepted by many horses who dislike thick mouthpieces.

Riding the horse in a pelham may help, provided you use double reins – and use them correctly. Double reins give a more precise action than roundings and a single rein. Many show producers put their young horses into pelhams from an early stage, as they find it helps them to learn to carry themselves and come off their forehands. It is vital that if you use a pelham or double bridle that the horse is ridden forwards and does not merely tuck his nose in and leave his back end trailing out behind.

The Schoolmasta (see the section on training aids) was designed to help with horses who snatch, pull or lean.

Napping

The easiest way to cure napping is not to let the habit start in the first place – which is not a lot of use if you happen to have bought a nappy youngster. For future reference, when you try a horse with a view to buying it, make sure that it will go in front of another one, going away from as well as towards home, and that it will go past its own gate. If you have been caught out or have made the mistake of putting a young horse under too much pressure too quickly, then of course you have no option but to sort out the problem, if necessary with professional help.

Napping can be due either to a lack of confidence or to the fact that the horse decides he would rather not go where you want him to. Always give a new horse of any age time to settle in to new surroundings and take him out in company before hacking out alone unless you are sure of your ability to give him confidence and keep him going forwards. Once he starts to settle on the yard and has been round a quiet route a couple of times with a companion, take him that way on his own.

Be prepared for the fact that at first he may be a bit spookier alone – again, keep him going forwards. Slopping along on a loose rein letting him stop and look at everything strange is asking for trouble. Always ride out round a circuit: never stop and retrace your steps, or one day the horse will decide that he would rather turn back a little earlier.

If you have schooled your horse from scratch, following the guidelines in this book, serious napping should not be a problem. However, you may find that one day your youngster decides that he is going to be the boss half of the partnership and that he would rather stay with his friends than leave the yard, or that you meet something he does not like the look of and does not want to go past.

Napping takes various forms. Some horses stop dead and refuse to budge in any direction, whilst others try and whip round. Others stop dead and threaten to rear, or actually stand up. Then there is the character who whips round and sets off for home at a great rate of knots; napping is bad enough, but napping coupled with brake failure is even worse!

The horse can only nap if he is not moving forwards, so the first requisite is a strong rider with good reactions and a steady nerve. Carry a schooling whip and if necessary wear spurs, and use them. The second you feel the horse hesitate, use your legs hard and give him a good smack on the girth. This is not the time for gentle squeezes and taps. Be prepared for him to shoot forwards and be ready to give with the reins so you do not jerk him in the mouth.

A standing martingale and a bit which gives greater steering power, such as a full cheek snaffle, helps with the horse who throws up his head and tries to whip round. If he does go round, turn him back the opposite way if possible so he does not make a complete circle. In other words, if he whips round to the left, turn him back to the right. Remember to use your legs and weight as a turning aid as much as the reins – setting your hand in a strong rein aid can provoke a horse to rear.

Sometimes the easiest way to deal with this is to disorientate the horse. Turn him in as tight circles as you can manage, then straighten and send him on with legs and stick.

The horse who stands still and says he is not going any further can be very time consuming. A helper with a lunge whip can provide the incentive he needs to go forwards, but must obviously be skilled enough to hit the horse, not the rider. Alternatively, a bucket of water thrown at the horse's backside from behind can provide the right element of surprise, especially for the horse who does not want to leave the yard. If your yard leads out on to a road, make sure you have someone standing at the gate telling you when it is safe to apply persuasion, or you run the risk of the horse shooting out in front of a car.

If you come to a dead halt with no helper in sight, and encouragement from legs and stick have no effect, you may have to sit it out. Keep the horse facing the direction in which you want him to go; he will eventually get as fed up as you are and decide to go.

That is when you get a little bit devious. Make him stand still for a few seconds and then push him on. You are the one who dictates when and where you go, not the horse.

Some horses are not content to stop and stand still. They go into reverse, which can be annoying or disconcerting depending on what is behind you. The classic, oft quoted advice for this situation is to back the horse into a prickly hedge so that the shock of it sends him forwards: fine if you happen to be in the right place at the right time, not so useful if there is a large ditch behind you rather than a hedge.

The good news is that horses have a strong instinct of self preservation and it is very rare that one will back itself into trouble. Obviously your sense of self-preservation needs to be just as strong, so if you are getting to the stage where things are looking dangerous the only sensible option is to get off and lead the horse out of harm's way. In general, you are more effective on the horse's back, but safety must come first.

This pony spooked at the photographer, but the rider is obeying the golden rule of looking straight ahead and they negotiated the grid successfully

Any horse can and probably will nap once. It only becomes a problem if it is allowed to become a habit – so if there are signs of that happening, get help. A strong, experienced rider who is used to dealing with young and/or problem horses can nip bad habits such as napping in the bud.

Spooking/shying

Some horses are naturally more spooky than others and will always remain so. However, if your horse starts spooking or shying for no apparent reason, get your vet to check his eyesight. If all is well, check that he is not getting too much to eat: hard feed combined with Spring grass can make a horse silly.

In general, the more you can ignore this sort of behaviour the less of a problem it will be. Hitting a horse for shying only confirms his opinion that there is something to be frightened of – and whilst it is infuriating to sit on a horse that spooks at a pole on the ground every time you go round the corner of the school, pretending it has not happened can sometimes be more effective than pushing the issue.

This does not mean that effective riding cannot help. Turn the horse's head away from whatever is worrying him rather than towards it; ride him in shoulder-in if his schooling has reached that stage. Try and get him used to strange things at home with a bit of 'police horse training' – lead him between and eventually over sheets of plastic on the ground, put coats over the rails of your schooling area and so on. If you have a show horse who spooks in the ring, turn your schooling area into a show ring by tying 'banners' and even balloons to the fences.

Traffic

Some horses accept everything from tractors to motor bikes right from day one; others are nervous of large or noisy vehicles or of ones that go past a bit too quickly, particularly if they have had a bad experience. The amount of traffic makes riding on the roads inherently risky, even on a mature, quiet horse, so do everything you can to make it safe. Avoid main roads and take a nervous or inexperienced horse out with a safe escort; wear a fluorescent and reflective belt or tabard to make you more visible and stay alert. Hacking might be relaxing, but becomes less so if you walk round the corner with your reins in loops and meet a tractor coming the other way.

Pick routes that allow you to ride two abreast for all or most of the time, and put the nervous horse on the inside of his escort, so that his nose is alongside the second horse's girth. This gives him a shield and means that potential hazards are past before he can react too much. As he begins to accept that things are not so frightening after all, move him up alongside his escort.

It is vital that whoever rides the nervous horse is confident enough to keep him going forwards but can stay relaxed. If the rider tenses, the horse will always sense it. With time, patience and expertise, most horses can be made safe to hack out. But if you know that yours may be worried by large or noisy vehicles, then take evasive action whenever you can. It is better to get out of the way into a gateway than risk an accident.

Chapter 12
Training Aids

Training aids – or gadgets, whatever you prefer to call them – are always controversial. Everyone knows that in an ideal world all horses could be trained according to classical principles and that no one would ever need to use them . . . but the real world is rather different. As we have said all the way along the line, doing it by the book is fine as long as the horse has read it too: sometimes you need an alternative approach to break through a communication problem and get you back on the right track.

To be frank, there is also a certain amount of snobbishness surrounding training aids. A lot of people who use them will not admit to it, because they think that this somehow casts a slur upon their abilities as a rider and/or trainer. The result is that when riders say they 'never use running reins' or 'don't believe in gadgets' it makes ordinary mortals feel guilty for resorting (or thinking of resorting) to them.

In the case of the beautifully made, perfectly balanced horse with a willingness to work, training aids are probably not needed by good riders. But the horse who finds something difficult or simply says 'Won't' can cause all sorts of problems even for the best riders, let along the average, competent horse person. You cannot trot round in circles, getting nowhere, forever. The time comes when you have to try a different approach.

The bottom line is that anything which works is worth using – as long as you follow certain rules. The first of these is that you make sure, if necessary with the help of your vet, that there is nothing physically wrong with your horse. If he is resisting or going badly because of discomfort or pain, then work of any description will only make things worse. Get his teeth, back, the fit of his tack and anything else that might be relevant checked before you go any further.

The second rule is that most training aids are only a means to an end. The reason for qualifying that statement with the word 'most' is that many people like to use martingales as standard pieces of tack, especially when jumping. But if you take the argument about how you define a training aid to its logical conclusion, then a martingale can be described as such. How else would you define something designed to prevent the horse raising his head above the angle of control?

In the same way, side reins (which were dealt with in the early part of this book) are training aids because they give a horse a contact to work up to on the lunge. To most people in Britain, they are a standard part of the lungeing equipment. On the Continent, the chambon is treated in the same manner and in some circumstances can be used to work a horse in a much more effective way. Here it is still treated with suspicion in some quarters – though having said that, a lot of trainers in the dressage world use it to great effect.

Draw reins, running reins and balancing reins should only be looked on as short-term aids. They are a means to an end, not an end in itself. A leading international dressage rider and trainer once described them as being rather like water wings – you put the latter on to help teach a child to swim, but your aim is for her to eventually swim unaided.

Training aids can sometimes help break through the communication barrier. If something is explained to you and you do not understand it, your teacher rephrases the information to try and make it clearer. Training aids can help you do the same: they can suggest to a horse that you want him to go in a certain way.

They are always a means of suggestion, never one of force. Strapping a horse's head down achieves nothing; using a training aid to ask him to lower his head and neck whilst you ride him forwards and encourage him to engage his quarters and hocks can achieve quite a lot when conventional methods have failed.

If you think a particular training aid might help you overcome a problem, but have never used it successfully, then if possible, get help from someone who has. Books such as this can try and cater for every eventuality, but can never take the place of that experienced 'eye on the ground'. An experienced trainer will often notice things that an inexperienced one may miss – so perhaps the best training aid anyone can use is a sympathetic expert!

Whatever training aid you use, err on the side of caution when you introduce it. Fit it loosely so that the horse can get used to the feel of it and what it is suggesting, then make any adjustments needed when you are confident he is not going to take fright and 'throw a wobbler'.

Unfortunately there is no such thing as a magic wand. A training aid is only as effective as the person using it. The classic example of this is draw reins: too many people are fooled by their horses tucking in their noses and fondly imagine that they are 'on the bit' even though their back ends are trailing out behind. Draw reins help to suggest the shape you want the horse to take, but only your effective riding can help him achieve it.

The difficulty with horses in general and training aids in particular is that there is no such thing as black and white. Trying to be dogmatic about the subject means you get nowhere: follow the guidelines suggested above, for the horse's benefit, and keep an open mind.

Martingales

A martingale gives extra control over a horse who throws his head up, especially if this move is preparatory to him bucking or napping. (Most people assume that horses put their heads down to buck. They do – but inevitably the first sign that this is going to happen is that the horse puts his head up.)

Whether you use a standing or a running martingale depends on your horse's way of going. The advantage of a standing martingale is that it has no contact with the bit and therefore will not put any pressure on the mouth; the disadvantage is that some horses will use it to lean against. This can lead to a build-up of muscle underneath the neck, exactly where you do not want it.

Because the reins go through the rings of a running martingale it affects the action of the bit. In some cases this can be an advantage in that it helps keep the bit on the bars of the mouth. It is also said to minimise the effects of a rider who finds it difficult to keep a steady contact, though this usually happens because he or she concentrates on keeping the hands still instead of following the movement of the horse's head when necessary. A possible disadvantage of the running martingale is that it can limit the rider's ability to open one or both reins to the side.

Whatever martingale you use, it must be fitted correctly. It is there to prevent the horse putting its head above the angle of control, not to pull it down. The classic advice on the standing martingale is that it should be adjusted so that it pushes up into the horse's gullet, but you may find that in practice it needs to be a hole shorter.

When a running martingale is correctly adjusted the rings will reach the horse's gullet. The textbook advice is to fasten it so that the rings can be pulled back to the withers – but this bases the fit on the shoulder, not the length of rein. If there is a kink in the reins when they are held normally and the horse's head carriage is relaxed, the martingale is too tight.

Market Harborough

The Market Harborough, which is something of a cross between a martingale and a rein, is very useful and much maligned. It is often categorised as being applicable to strong horses, but its range of uses is much wider and if it is correctly adjusted, there is nothing severe about it. It starts off like a martingale, fastening at the girth, then splits into two arms which each have a small clip at the end. These arms go through the bit rings and the clips fasten on to small D-rings on specially made reins.

The beauty of the Market Harborough is that it is operated by the horse, not the rider. If the horse goes correctly, it has no effect at all, but if he raises his head too high the martingale reins come into effect and exert a downward pressure on the bit and therefore the bars of the mouth. As soon as the horse lowers his head, he is rewarded because the pressure ceases.

As with all training aids, adjust it loosely to start with. Make sure that it is never adjusted so tightly that the martingale rein comes into effect before the direct one, or the horse will not be rewarded for yielding to its action. If the horse shows any tendency to rear, push your hands right forwards so that the pressure on the bars of his mouth is

The Market Harborough is operated by the horse, not the rider, and only comes into effect when he raises his head above the acceptable angle.

removed and he is less likely to go over backwards. (see the section on draw and running reins, below).

The Market Harborough is allowed in British Show Jumping Association horse classes, whereas draw, running and balancing reins can only be used outside the ring.

Draw and running reins

These are the most commonly used – and unfortunately, abused – training aids. The names are often used as if they were interchangeable, but strictly speaking they have distinct fittings and uses. Draw reins start at the girth, pass between the front legs, through the bit rings to the rider's hands. Running reins fasten to the girth at each side under the flaps, then pass through the bit rings and back to the hands. In both cases, the training rein should run from the inside to the outside to avoid a squeezing effect. It should also be used in conjunction with an ordinary, direct rein.

Draw reins, shown here, have a more definite lowering effect than running reins, which go from under the saddle flaps, through the bit rings and back to the rider's hands.

Draw reins have a distinct lowering effect on the horse's head and are generally stronger in their action. Running reins ask him to bring in his nose but do not have such a lowering action – so the variation you choose depends on the individual horse and what you are trying to achieve. Draw reins are more likely to make the horse overbend – though against that, some expert practitioners use them precisely to make the horse overbend. Top show jumpers, some of whom are masters in the art of using draw reins, want to stretch the horse's topline so that he uses himself to the maximum over fences.

It is sometimes said that draw reins in uneducated hands are like razor blades in the hands of a monkey, but to be honest you could say that about any training aid – or even any bit. Certainly it is important for the inexperienced rider, or one who is unsure about their use, to get help from someone who is knowledgeable about their application and has the successes to prove it. More snobbery is provoked by their use than just about any other device: the ultimate answer is to point out to your critics that running reins are a) used in the Spanish Riding School and b) were invented by the English master of equitation, the Duke of Newcastle, in the 17th century.

They should be used only to suggest that the horse adopts the desired head carriage, not to force his head down, and should only be used with a snaffle. Most important of all, the principle of leg into hand must apply – too many people use them to get their horses' heads down and/or in and forget to ride forwards, so that the hindlegs are trailing out behind and the horses are going nowhere. It is also important to reward the horse when he gives to their action by immediately riding on the direct rein only. The way to achieve this is to hold the direct rein and the running/draw rein as if you were holding the reins of a double bridle, with the direct rein as the top (snaffle) rein and the running rein as the bottom (curb) rein. Bring the running rein into play to ask the horse to yield, making sure that you are riding him forwards from the leg, and as he gives to you, make sure you give to him – release the contact on the running rein and ride him only on the direct one.

Some trainers like to use draw reins when hacking out on horses who goggle and spook and generally fall over their own feet because they are too busy looking round. However, the Market Harborough often does the same job and, because it is operated by the horse and not the rider, is a preferable alternative. If draw reins are used, it is important that the horse's way of going is sufficiently established for him to understand that he must go forwards. It is also important that the rider is skilled in their use: a green horse and a green pair of hands on the reins is a pretty dire combination. The horse *must* know and understand the basics before you use them: they are an aid to communication, not a shortcut to getting an 'advanced outline'.

From the safety point of view, it is a good idea to fasten a spare stirrup leather round the horse's neck and to thread the draw reins underneath them. It will not interfere with their action, as long as it is not too tight, and will remove the risk of the draw reins dangling between the forelegs and the horse tripping over them. Jumping in draw or running reins is not recommended unless you are in the same calibre as David Broome or the Whitakers!

They should only be regarded as a short-term measure: if the horse only goes nicely when you are riding him in running reins then you are kidding yourself and should go back to basics with some expert help. Leading international dressage rider Richard Davison summed it up beautifully when he said that draw reins were like water wings – you might use them when you were teaching a child to swim, but not on a permanent basis.

Once the horse understands what you are asking him, their use should be limited to occasional 'reminders'. If they help with the inattentive or spooky horse out hacking, then use them with the neckstrap and knot them on the neck so that they can be picked up as necessary. Be very, very careful about using them on a horse who has shown a tendency to rear (or even one who threatens to go up). If you do not release both running and direct reins as soon as the horse starts to rear, there is a real danger that he will go over backwards because he does not have enough freedom of his head and neck.

The Abbot-Davies Balancing Rein.

When Peter Abbot-Davies first developed his balancing rein in the 1970s, it quickly became the centre of controversy – mainly because the original system involved

The Abbot-Davies balancing rein is said to help build up the horse's top line.

connecting the horse's tail to his mouth via a sheepskin covered rope and the balancing rein. Surprising as this may sound, it is a theory which goes way back in history to the ancient Egyptians – Rameses III used it when driving a two-in-hand chariot.

Although horses seem to accept this with equanimity, the company which markets the Abbot-Davies now says that it is not essential and that it can be used in the normal riding position right from the start. (It can also be used for lungeing.) The rein uses a system of pulleys and encourages the horse to stretch round and down – in fact the instructions say that the horse must be worked with the head and neck overbent for the first three months so that he builds up muscles which, when the rein is removed, will help him find it easier to work on the bit.

It is important that the balancing rein is only used for short periods to start with to avoid over-stressing the muscles, and that the horse is ridden forwards. The manu-facturers say that the hands must be more active and that the legs must be as active as the hands so that the horse is not allowed to lean on the bit. More information is available from Davies, Benaki and Co Ltd, The Balancing Rein Stud, Roade, Northants NN7 2LX.

The Schoolmasta

The Schoolmasta is a training aid designed to help correct headstrong horses or those who lean on the bit or overbend. It can also be useful for lungeing, as it is not 'fixed' like side reins and the horse can bend to either side, and to introduce young horses to the idea of a contact whilst they are standing in the stable. As with the Market Harborough, its strength lies in the fact that it is operated by the horse, not the rider.

It comprises adjustable reins with a rolled connecting strap and a specially designed and strengthened numnah with a pulley. Basically, the Schoolmasta reins are designed to 'take the strain', enabling the rider to keep a light hand and secure seat. The manufacturers say it should be fitted on the longest adjustment to start with and the horse should be lunged in it so that he gets used to the feel. Once this has been accomplished, the Schoolmasta reins 'should be progressively shortened as the horse relaxes until the desired head carriage has been achieved.'

Obviously the time taken will depend on the individual horse; it is recommended that when it is first introduced, it should not be used for longer than half hour periods at a time. Once the horse is going correctly, it will have no effect – it only comes into play if he leans, pulls or whatever. For more information, contact the manufacturers: Masta Horse Clothing Co. Ltd, Crosland Moor Mills, Huddersfield HD4 5AH.

The chambon

On the Continent, the chambon – which is used only for loose schooling or lungeing – is considered to be not a gadget but an essential part of the basic equipment. It encourages the horse to lower his head and neck, stretch his whole topline and thus move with a loose, swinging back and rhythmic stride. Horses who find it easy to evade side reins by tucking in their noses and coming behind the bit will often work better in a chambon.

It starts at the girth, like a martingale, then splits into two cord or rolled leather reins. These pass through small rings on each end of a short, padded strap which goes over the poll, then go down the sides of the horse's face and finally clip to the bit rings. It *must* be fitted very loosely when it is introduced and the person lungeing must be capable of keeping the horse going forwards.

The chambon is a particular favourite of many show jumpers, because it encourages the use of muscles along the neck, back and quarters and promotes suppleness, but it can be beneficial for any horse who tends to 'come back' at his rider and tighten in his neck. It is essential, of course, to check that he is not doing this because of rider error (which usually means too much hand and too little leg) and to rectify this if necessary. Even if incorrect riding is to blame, the chambon can still help by showing the horse that it is more comfortable to work in a different way.

There are, of course, many other training aids. Some, such as the de Gogue (a more advanced version of the chambon which can be used for ridden work as well as loose schooling and lungeing and whose use must be demonstrated to you by an expert) have long and impeccable pedigrees and can achieve excellent results in the hands of skilled users. Others fall into the 'five minute wonder' category and fail to prove themselves. Whilst there is always room for good ideas, the ones discussed here should cover most eventualities.

There is no guarantee that what works for one horse will work for another: and as every training aid depends ultimately on the rider's ability to use it, it is also true that what works for one rider may not work for another! Keep your approach to training as simple as possible and if you hit a problem, get help. If your helper has proven success and recommends the use of a particular training aid, then try it.

Chapter 13
Taking on an Ex-racehorse

If you want to buy a young Thoroughbred horse, then you may well be considering one that has come out of racing. Recent figures show that up to 96 per cent of those horses which are bred for racing do not make it to the track, which obviously means that an enormous number of horses are available to be re-routed to other careers. They can end up as 'racing rejects' for many reasons; some are simply not fast enough, some lack the necessary urge that makes winners want to be in front of everything else and some are physically unable to stand up to the rigours of training and racing.

A sound horse is obviously the best bet, but a lot of horses whose legs show signs of not standing up to racing will cope with hacking, dressage and even show jumping. If you are prepared to take a risk and have the horse vetted by a good vet who knows exactly what you want him to do, it may be worth considering.

There is an awful lot of rubbish talked about ex-racehorses. You will often hear people say that they are always excitable and never have any brakes, when in fact they are just as much individuals as any other breed. You can find quiet Thoroughbreds just as you can find fizzy cobs; what you have to keep in mind are the common denominators of the breed.

Thoroughbreds bred with Flat racing in mind are bred for speed, and their conformation reflects that. They are not bred to go in a collected outline (though they can be schooled to do so by a good rider) and are usually lightweight. Thoroughbreds bred for National Hunt racing are bigger and more substantial than Flat horses – in fact the National Hunt sales rings are a favourite hunting ground for buyers from many other disciplines, so they are often more expensive than Flat horses.

A Thoroughbred may well be kind and as sensible as any other young horse, but it will usually be sensitive (both mentally and physically) and have quick reactions. If the horse is handled and worked correctly, these characteristics can work in your favour. If you misjudge, they can work against you.

Thoroughbreds are thin skinned and fine coated. Whereas a half-bred horse or cob will probably be a good doer and have the sort of coat that protects him from the weather, a Thoroughbred will usually need more food and more rugs, thus making him more expensive to keep. There are exceptions, and plenty of Thoroughbreds that come out of racing and are then let down on good spring grass soon put on weight and no longer look like lean racing machines. But if you anticipate higher feed bills in autumn and winter you will not get a nasty surprise when a 16hh Thoroughbred seems to need twice as much hard feed as a 15hh cob. All in all, you have to be prepared to cosset a Thoroughbred, especially if it has just come from the racing world and has been stabled and rugged up for most of the time.

Ex-racehorses have pluses and minuses. Let us start with the minuses – not that any of them would present an insurmountable problem for a competent handler and rider.

Racehorses are broken in a different way from other horses. They are started as yearlings and the trainer's main aim is to produce a horse that can gallop faster than its rivals. The breaking process is simple and usually fairly rapid; the yearling will be accustomed to tack, long reined, backed and will then get on with the job of training.

A three-year-old Thoroughbred mare straight out of racing.

Trainers in the racing world are not usually bothered about getting the horse to bend or to carry itself in a correct outline, whereas the 'ordinary' trainer works the horse right from the start with the idea of establishing balance, working from the leg into the hand and establishing a good outline. It has to be said that some trainers do get their horses to accept the bit and bend, reasoning that a horse which is arguing with its rider will lose ground – but some do not.

The same mare after she had been turned out and let down for three months.

The racehorse that was broken with the principles of balance, rhythm and acceptance of the bit in mind will have a far better top line than the one whose trainer followed the 'get on it and gallop' philosophy. The horse from the latter category will probably have a weak topline and will have developed strong muscles underneath the neck, exactly where you do not want them. Correct work will rectify this, but it will take time.

Flat racehorses are at their career peaks as two and three-year-olds, at a time when they are cutting teeth and perhaps in a permanent state of discomfort. Some trainers do all they can to minimise this by getting their horses' mouths checked and attended to every six months by a specialist horse dentist or vet. Others are not so bothered and unfortunately follow the 'if it throws its head up, put a running martingale on' school of thought.

Again, time and correct handling can sort out this sort of thing, but you have to be prepared to be patient and to take the horse right back to basics. Treat it as you would an unbroken three-year-old: get its mouth checked and sorted out, re-bit it and go back

Bella, a six-year-old ex-racehorse who raced on the Flat. She has lovely paces and should do well in dressage.

to lungeing with side reins and so on. Racehorses are nearly always ridden in loose ring snaffles, so 'gobby' ones may need to be mouthed with a breaking bit with keys on before the loose ring or whatever other type of snaffle you decide to use is introduced once more.

Do not make the mistake of thinking that you have bought a racehorse and equating this with another species. A racehorse is still a horse and if you treat it with quiet confidence and sufficient respect, it should respond. Being in a racing yard will even have given you some pluses: for a start, you have bought a horse that is bred specifically to perform and should possess agility, stamina and a degree of speed – all ideal attributes for the event horse, for example.

Racehorses are usually good on the roads, because they are used to being ridden in traffic. However, they are ridden out in company, not alone – so whilst your ex-racehorse may walk round the roads with the aplomb of a much older horse, do not expect him to do the same on his own until he has settled in and you have established basic communications. He might be just as good by himself as when he is with a companion, but it would be a mistake to assume it.

Because they are well handled in the stable, racehorses are usually good to tie up and shoe and often to clip as well. A three-year-old out of racing will usually accept many of the things you would normally only expect in an older animal: if you are used to horses that are at least six or seven, it can be quite a shock discovering all that you have to teach a real juvenile!

Bella has come above the bit and hollowed her back, creating a picture of resistance. This is the time when you wish horses could read books . . .

Sometimes the most difficult thing about taking on an ex-racehorse is buying one. Racing is a business and trainers do not have the time or the inclination to deal with a line of strangers interrupting their yard routine and trying horses when the only facilities are High Streets and gallops. The traditional and accepted way of selling racehorses is through bloodstock sales – and buying at auction is nerve racking unless you understand what happens and how to do it or have someone with you who does.

Read the sales catalogues carefully. They will contain a section on sales conditions which states the terms sellers and buyers must comply with. For instance, most auctioneers stipulate that a horse with a recognised stable vice – weaving, crib biting and wind sucking, though not necessarily box walking – has to be declared as such. Stable vices are quite common in racehorses, mainly because they are kept in an artificial environment once they are in training. They are usually stabled except when at exercise, so may spend 23 hours out of 24 in their boxes. Most trainers could not care less what their horses do in their spare time if they come up with the goods, so do not look on weaving, cribbing, wind sucking etc with as much concern as the 'ordinary' rider might.

A horse either has a vice or does not. 'Seen to weave' might mean that it waves its head from side to side a few times when it sees someone approaching with a feed, or it might mean that it sways like a top and does the Fandango with its front feet all the time it is stabled. If it is declared to have a vice, you cannot return it if the habit turns out to be worse than you expected.

Later in the same schooling session. Bella is soft and rounded and the picture is one of harmony.

The one thing you have to take a risk on at auction is a horse's temperament, though your own observations will help you pinpoint the obviously nervous animal or the horse that tries to take a lump out of anyone who walks into its box. This does not mean that either the auctioneers or the sellers are trying to pull the wool over anyone's eyes, simply that a trainer does not give two hoots about anything other than a horse's ability and will cope with or put up with undesirable traits that people who keep horses for pleasure would find impossible.

Finally, remember when you bid that you are bidding in guineas, not pounds – so 1,000 guineas means you are paying £1,100. In some cases, you may also have to add

VAT to that, and a reasonable price often does not seem quite so reasonable when you work out seventeen and a half per cent of your bid and add it on.

An alternative way of finding an ex-racehorse is to buy through a reputable dealer. Some trainers will sell their straight, easy horses to a dealer because it saves them an auctioneer's commission and the expense and hassle of having to send a horse to the sales. They will probably still send the dodgy or difficult ones to the sales, because good dealers do not want that sort of horse unless it is so talented that nothing else matters. From the trainer's point of view, selling to a dealer is quick and easy – it is someone they know who comes on to the yard, looks at the horse and says yes or no.

From the average buyer's point of view, buying from a dealer is far less of a risk than buying at auction. The dealer will have assessed the horse's temperament and be able to give you a good idea of where its future lies and the work that needs to be done on it. You will also be able to try the horse – though do not expect it to feel anything but green and wobbly unless the dealer has done some work on it. Most important, you will be able to have it vetted for a particular purpose.

Once you get your now ex-racehorse home, do not assume that because he was in training you can gaily jump straight on and set about re-schooling work. You have a far better chance of success if you turn him out, let him relax and unwind and take the edge off his fitness. The average rider's idea of a very fit horse is radically different from a trainer's definition. This breathing space gives the horse chance to get to know his surroundings and both of you have the opportunity to get to know each other. It also means that you can get his mouth and teeth checked and if necessary seen to before you put a bit in his mouth.

Index